GENTLEMAN TRAIN ROBBER

AMAZING STORIES

GENTLEMAN TRAIN ROBBER
The Daring Escapades of Bill Miner

HISTORY/BIOGRAPHY

by Stan Sauerwein

PUBLISHED BY ALTITUDE PUBLISHING CANADA LTD.
1500 Railway Avenue, Canmore, Alberta T1W 1P6
www.altitudepublishing.com
1-800-957-6888

Extreme care has been taken to ensure that all information presented in
this book is accurate and up to date. Neither the author nor the
publisher can be held responsible for any errors.

Publisher	Stephen Hutchings
Associate Publisher	Kara Turner
Editor	Dianne Smyth
Digital Photo Coloring	Bryan Pezzi

We acknowledge the financial support of the Government
of Canada through the Book Publishing Industry Development
Program (BPIDP) for our publishing activities.

Altitude GreenTree Program 🌲
Altitude Publishing will plant twice as many trees as were used
in the manufacturing of this product.

Cataloging in Publication Data

Sauerwein, Stan, 1952-
Gentleman train robber : the daring escapades of
Bill Miner / Stan Sauerwein. -- US ed.

(Amazing stories)
Includes bibliographical references.
ISBN 1-55265-124-X

1. Miner, Bill, 1846-1913. 2. Brigands and robbers--Canada--Biography.
3. Brigands and robbers--United States--Biography. 4. Train robberies--History.
I. Title. II. Series: Amazing stories (Canmore, Alta.)

HV6248.M55S27 2006   364.15'52'092   C2006-900297-5

Amazing Stories® is a registered trademark of Altitude Publishing Canada Ltd.

Printed and bound in Canada by Friesens
2 4 6 8 9 7 5 3 1

"Hands up!"
William A. Miner

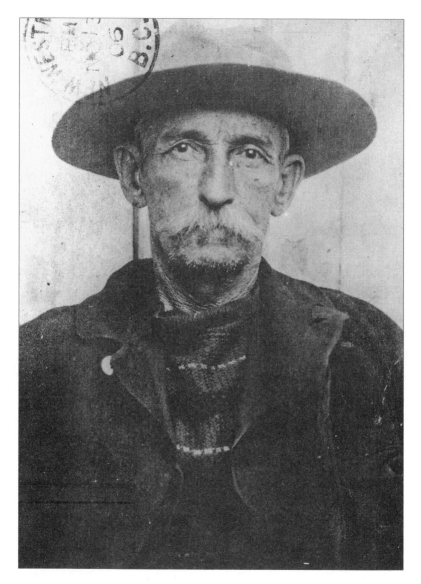

Bill Miner

Contents

Prologue

"Hands up!"

Nate Scott felt the sudden pressure of a fist on his shoulder and the unmistakable threat of a gun barrel pressed to his temple. He raised his arms and slowly turned to face a black hood and the steely-blue eyes of a bandit. This had never happened before. The Canadian Pacific Railway (CPR) Continental Express bound through the Rocky Mountains for Vancouver had never been robbed. The engineer could have frantically killed the throttle, perhaps sending his off-balance assailant lurching from the engine into the fog, but he didn't. He was a married man and he had no intention of being a hero. Besides, the bandit's handgun was held in deadly aim, and from behind a crudely sewn mask, the orders the bandit gave were cold and certain. "I want you to stop the train at Silverdale crossing. Do what you are told and not a hair of your head will be harmed," the bandit warned in a soft southern drawl.

"I am at your service," the engineer answered carefully, turning back to his work. He had to crane his neck to see forward. Cutting through a dense fog, the yellow beam of the engine's headlamp was useless to him. It barely exposed the thick crowding edge of forest whipping by the train as it

steamed through heavy mist toward the coast, but Nate knew Silverdale was just ahead. He eased back on the throttle and let the train slow toward the siding between Mission Junction and Whonnock.

Once he'd brought the train to a wheezing stop, Nate turned around. His assailant was pushing the train's fireman, Harry Freeman, from the cab. Another bandit now had a rifle pointed squarely in the engineer's face. "Uncouple the train at the express car, please."

The fireman complied immediately. He stumbled in the darkness toward the rear of the train just as the brakeman, Bill Abbott, poked his head from between the cars. Why had the Express made an unscheduled stop? A delay would play hell with their schedule.

"Get back inside unless you want your head blown off, and be quick," Freeman's guard shouted.

Abbott popped back inside, gulping air. "Robbery," he shouted to dozing passengers! "We're being robbed!" The brakeman fumbled his way down the aisle, shooting furtive glances to the dark passenger car windows. "Hide your valuables and make it quick. We're being robbed!"

Chapter 1
The Road to San Quentin

t wouldn't be fair to say his childhood made him a criminal. That would suggest Ezra's mother didn't do a proper job raising the fatherless boy. Nor could one say Ezra left home and, because of bad luck, fell into a life of crime. From an early age, Ezra never really had a "home" to leave. Home sort of left him. And, as far as crime was concerned, stealing came naturally.

After his father died, Ezra's "home" sifted through his mother's fingers in auctions. It drifted away in land sales and claims on the estate. From then on, it was lost to the 10-year-old boy. Ezra was born in Onondaga, Michigan, two days after Christmas in 1846. Though he grew up in other parts of the agricultural heartland of Michigan, he always thought of the clapboard house shared with his brothers and sister as the closest thing to home he'd ever had. As he grew up, that tiny town and the people living there became a symbol for all the might-have-been the world had taken from him.

Before Ezra's father died of a brain disease on November 1, 1856, he had built a small "paper" fortune as an urban landowner. Some of the property was even held in Ezra's name as the start of his son's own real estate empire. But when Joseph Miner suddenly passed away, the family learned that owning title to lots in Clinton, where they were then living, was a shaky foundation for wealth. Vacant lots did nothing but create a tax bill unless they were bought and sold for a profit. Ezra's mother had no skills in that department.

The tragedy of Joseph's death put the Miners on a fast track to poverty. Ezra's older brother Henry worked as a store clerk to help pay the bills, but it didn't help much. Ezra's mother, Harriet, was forced to sell their properties as a stopgap to avoid the poorhouse. The family fortunes rapidly declined anyway, even to the point where Harriet had to call on charity to support Ezra, his sister Mary Jane, and their little brother Benjamin. And there were rumours that a civil war was brewing between the industrial north and the secessionist south. People said it was sure to happen if Abraham Lincoln was elected president. Harriet realized that, in order to survive, she had to find another husband. More to the point, she knew if she didn't act quickly, there might not be many healthy and able suitors available.

Harriet decided to look west. California was the continental limit of an escape from imminent civil war. She may have also believed there were plenty of wealthy gold miners eager to find a wife in California, even if she was a widow with four children. So, in 1860, she trekked westward with her brood to Yankee Jims, leaving only Henry behind. The first settlers had congregated at Yankee Jims, California, in 1850. The richest surface diggings of gold discovered up to that time in American history had been found in California. Unfortunately, that was 10 years before Harriet pointed her wagon toward the Pacific.

She and her tiny flock settled north of Auburn, but life was no easier for Harriet and her brood even though Henry continued to send his mother subsistence money for a time. The romantic notion of wealthy and independent gold miners was just that. The time when lone prospectors could strike it rich around Yankee Jims was long over. Only the avaricious corporations were growing wealthy from the muscle and sweat of grumbling miners. When Harriet arrived in California, she found her future marriage prospects were all laborers, barely surviving on meagre wages themselves. Ezra passed through his puberty in an environment of need. He joined the miners in their toil when barely in his teens, but at 16 Ezra decided life had to be better than that. It had to hold more than a pick to swing or the nozzle of a hydraulic mining hose to wrestle. Barely old enough to shave, Ezra followed the lure of easy money and turned to crime.

In June 1863, while still only 16 years old, Ezra was

charged with horse theft, a transgression generally considered more despicable than murder in the west. James Keller and young Ezra, who by then was calling himself William Miner, were jailed on charges of grand larceny for stealing stock from a prominent Los Angeles County ranchero. The charges against them were dropped in December, six months later, but the time spent behind bars was reason enough for Ezra to reconsider a life as a desperado. In February 1864, he made a push toward the straight and narrow. Ezra's brother wrote the family to announce he'd enlisted in the Michigan infantry for a three-year stint. Ezra told his mother that what was good enough for Henry was good enough for him. Harriet didn't argue. Anything, even the prospect of having her son sent east to fight the Rebel Army, was better than watching Ezra march to the noose as a horse thief.

In late April, Ezra lied about his age to army recruiters. Recruit No. 23 in Company L of the Second Regiment of California Cavalry Volunteers gave his name as William A. Miner and his occupation as mine laborer. Bill (Ezra) had an average build and wasn't very tall (5 feet 8 inches). But, he was clean-cut, affable, and outgoing. Bill's blue eyes constantly sparkled with a mischievous glint, and his gift for conversation helped him get along well with the officers. Though the rest of his Company was sent to a hot dusty frontier outpost at Camp Relief in Utah, Bill got assigned to a more civilized posting at Camp Union in Sacramento.

Military life was easier for soldiers in California, but army discipline didn't agree with Bill.

He balked at the duties he was assigned. In his mind, the army was no better than the uncaring mining companies when it came to consideration for a man's welfare. His own experience, coupled with letters from Henry, soon made Bill rue his decision to join up. Henry had contracted dysentery after enlisting and related horror stories about the substandard medical care he was receiving. Henry subsequently died in August. By July, Bill was fed up with army life. He recklessly deserted his post, made his way back to his mother in Placer County, and found work in the mines.

Miraculously, when army administrators inquired as to recruit No. 23's whereabouts, Bill's commander could find no record of the boy. If he had, Bill may have served time in the army stockade and been on a different path for the rest of his life.

There was a rebellious side to Bill's character, as evidenced by his desertion. But he may also have resented the U.S. government for not taking proper care of his brother during his illness. In addition, he'd seen many examples of miners being victimized by rich mining companies. Perhaps he had felt that victimization himself. He grew to hate the power that corporations had over the workingman during the 1800s. It pushed him toward an attitude that could be described as "socialist," and may have prompted him to act out his revenge on large corporations through robbery.

Or, perhaps it was just the influence of unseemly men and women on a naïve youngster in California gold country. By the time he was 18, Bill's morals were greasy and he'd taken up with a "woman of bad character" in Sacramento County. Her prompting may have encouraged him to find a foolproof way of maintaining his affair with her, because in December he held up his mine employer for $300.

Bill was caught, but misplaced kindness soon let him off. His employer was convinced the older woman and her loose morals had led the courteous youth astray. As with most others who encountered Bill, the mine boss failed to realize that the young man was a talented manipulator. Bill could look quite contrite while he secretly harbored plans to the opposite effect. Besides, he'd gotten a taste of the shady life and he liked it.

Miner was already a habitual criminal because soon after that lucky brush with the law, he was ready to try a different "trick." He'd worked out a scheme to get to San Francisco where he planned to sample the brothels his mining cohorts had described. To do that, he knew he needed proper clothes and walking-around money. On December 28, 1865, Bill celebrated his 19th birthday by taking a train to the nearby town of Newcastle. He hired a horse from the livery stable, promising to return it that afternoon, and then promptly headed for Auburn. Arriving that evening, Bill went to a clothing store and waited until it was about to close. The impatient store clerk watched as the last customer of the day carefully picked out an expensive $90 suit. He reluctantly helped the young man try it on. It fit well, and to the clerk's relief Bill was pleased with his selection.

After the clerk wrapped the purchase in paper, Bill confessed he had no money with him. The Placer County treasurer was holding it, Bill said. He invented a tale of an inheritance and politely asked if the clerk would be willing to accompany him to the treasurer's home after he closed the shop to collect full payment. Bill even helped the clerk, who was by then very eager to lock up the shop. On the walk to the treasurer's street, the young man engaged the clerk in pleasant conversation, giving no indication of what was about to happen. When they reached a secluded alley near the treasurer's house, however, all that changed. Bill roughly shoved the clerk into the dark alley and drew a pistol.

"I'm on the rob," he growled, "so please give me your money."

The assault took the clerk completely by surprise, not only because of the robber's age, but also because of his polite manner and confidence. The young man was clean-cut and had a ruddy complexion that could have been earned by working outdoors. He looked the part of the God-fearing orphan he'd claimed to be. When the clerk told Bill he had no money, Bill took the suit and then the clerk's gold watch for good measure. Under threat of death, he told the clerk to wait 20 minutes before alerting the police.

Oddly, the clerk did as he was told. In recounting the

details of the robbery to his employer, the clerk confessed managing the delay was difficult, since he had to count out the time on his fingers. Even as the comical story was being retold, the liveryman from Newcastle arrived in Auburn on a quest for his missing horse. The clerk's and the liveryman's description of the young man who'd robbed them matched. Local police officers were soon combing the Auburn countryside for the sweet-talking desperado and they had a pretty good idea what their quarry looked like. Unfortunately for them, Bill had already fled unseen to Yankee Jims.

On January 4, 1866, Bill put the rest of his plan into action. He went to Forest Hill, a town a little less than two miles from Yankee Jims, hired another horse, and then headed for San Francisco. Bill's imagination was crowded with stories he'd heard about the wild coastal city. When he shared these stories with a waiter two years his junior at Stockton's Weber House, Bill found himself the first of many gullible traveling partners.

John Sinclair brought along his savings. When they arrived in San Francisco, Bill sold his two stolen horses for a bankroll of his own. For two weeks the young men did their best to prove that all those tales about the Barbary Coast's bordellos, saloons, and gambling houses were true. On January 19, they used the last of their money to hire horses, complete with saddle and tack, from a livery in Oakland. Once again, Bill promised to return them that afternoon and the stable keeper believed him. Of course, Bill had no more intention of doing that than he had the last two times. He quickly managed to sell the horses to a constable in Georgetown and the two boys turned back toward Stockton. Bill must have marveled at how easy it was to steal, even from a lawman, because after walking for two days he decided to flag down a wagon, about 19 miles outside of Stockton, at Johnson's Ferry.

At first, the man they intended to rob thought the young bandits' command to give them his wagon was a joke, but when Sinclair drew his revolver, the victim dropped the reins and raised his hands to indicate he would comply. Bill noted the gesture. "That's it, hands up and now please haul out your money." When the victim told the boys he had none, Sinclair cursed, called him a "damned liar" and demanded the man "shell out" or suffer the consequences. Their victim relented and turned over $80, whining about how the robbery was going to ruin his plan to buy new boots. Miner took pity on him and returned $10. He then told his victim not to report the robbery or they'd return to settle the score with a murder, even if it took them 10 years.

Using the wagon team, the two youths galloped to Woodbridge, almost 15 miles north of Stockton, as if a posse already had their scent. Since Sinclair owned a gun and Bill was unarmed, Bill spent part of his victim's boot money on a weapon. Then the pair checked into a Woodbridge hotel, thinking they were safely anonymous.

Their victim, however, was livid at having to walk to

Stockton. He ignored Miner's threat and reported the robbery, providing accurate descriptions of both men. That same evening, the Oakland constabulary sent a telegraph bulletin to neighboring towns concerning two horses stolen from their town's livery stable. The perpetrators' descriptions matched exactly. With a fast canvass for witnesses, the Stockton lawmen learned that two boys were seen riding bareback toward Woodbridge. It was a simple matter of looking for the horses in Woodbridge, and before sunrise the next morning the Stockton deputy sheriff tugged the boys from their beds and put them under arrest.

With an example of swift frontier justice, the deputy sheriff moved his bound prisoners into the Stockton jail by that afternoon. A prompt preliminary hearing the next day committed Miner and Sinclair to trial at the next sitting of the county court, which was not expected until late the following month. Neither boy could front the $1000 bail the judge required, so they were returned to the Stockton lockup.

The wait suited the young desperadoes because it gave them time to engineer an escape. By February 20, they'd managed to dislodge bolts from the cell window and had used the metal to dig a tunnel under the wall. Unbeknownst to them, however, the jailers suspected as much. The following day as they moved Miner and Sinclair to separate cells, the lawmen promptly discovered the escape hole. When Bill was confronted with the evidence, he showed his dry wit. If they knew, he complained, why had they waited so long? For heaven sake, he'd nearly broken a tooth pulling a bolt from the window casing.

Miner's luck quickly turned worse. On March 7, he was charged with grand theft for the Newcastle heist and on March 8 for the Forest Hill theft. On March 10, he and Sinclair were charged with the Stockton horse theft, as well. Bill had done a good job of building a bad reputation. Because of the other charges he was facing, the men had separate trials. Sinclair was given three years in San Quentin for his short partnership in crime with the hooligan, William A. Miner.

Defended by James H. Budd on March 10, Miner was convicted of the Johnson's Ferry robbery and sentenced to three years in San Quentin, as well. After a tongue-lashing from the judge, Miner only smiled. An officer of the court asked him what he found so humorous. Miner told him he was surprised that he had received such a short sentence, especially after uttering a murder threat. Miner's lawyer was taken aback by the young man's stoicism. Before Bill was escorted from the court, Budd told him that if there should ever be an opportunity, he'd do anything in his power to help him. Bill never forgot that offer.

On April 5, 1866, Miner and Sinclair were processed into San Quentin penitentiary. On admission, the prison guards gave Bill a careful physical examination. They noted he had a small scar on his forehead, pock mocks on his face, and several primitive tattoos including a *VA* on the back of his left hand and a five-pointed star on his right forearm. Over the years, Bill's poor judgment resulted in him adding to these body decorations.

San Quentin had improved since it was first established 12 years earlier, but it was still a hellhole. Prior to 1849, prisons in California consisted of local lock-ups, but with the Gold Rush the area had been overrun by desperate characters and a better system was needed. Authorities first tried using ships as an alternative to building prisons. In 1851, California state officials decided to lease out convicts to local contractors in order to save the public purse their incarceration expenses.

General Mariana Vallejo and General James M. Estelle were the first to take over the responsibility for felons. They bought an old barkentine sailing ship and signed a contract to manage 50 convicts for the penal authorities. Their three-masted prison ship was anchored off Point Quentin on July 14, 1852. The two generals also used the money they had to construct a flat stone fortress on land nearby. Space for additional prisoners meant more money. However, their efforts as prison managers were incredibly inept and ill fated.

The two generals crammed the barkentine with criminals of all kinds and both sexes while they built their fortress onshore. The prison ship was a floating torture chamber for its captives. It lacked sanitation and disease was rampant. Social misfits supervised the convicts. To relieve the boredom of their duty, the guards participated in drinking bouts, gambling, rape, and brutality.

When their Spanish Cell Block was finally erected, the generals moved their prison operation ashore. But instead of improved living conditions, the prisoners' lot worsened. The Spanish Cell Block was a badly designed sieve. The number of fleeing prisoners became so significant that, in 1854, the state legislature decreed that a ten-foot wall be built around the fortress. Even then, the prison couldn't hold its prisoners, so the generals turned over the facility's operations to a man named J. F. McCauley. His assignment was to operate the prison at a profit, but he failed just as miserably. Finally, bowing to electoral pressure, the state's politicians assumed control of the prisons in 1860.

The state's idea was to crack down on the convicts with even more brutality in order to put an end to the regular routine of escapes, but increased brutality only resulted in more violence and more escape attempts. In 1864, the prisoners were so desperate to get away that they rioted — seized Warden T.N. Machin and escaped — *en masse*. It took an army of citizens to corner the convicts at Ross' Landing and return them to prison. Machin reacted to the prison break with a reign of terror that lasted for the next 25 years. He instituted a policy of shaving the hair from half a prisoner's scalp to make an escapee easily identifiable. Machin had a jute mill and a brick plant built on the prison grounds where he could extract slave labor. Exhausted prisoners, he believed, were less likely to attempt escape.

Warden Machin turned San Quentin into a hell of iron

discipline where antisocial men had their spirits and bodies broken as a means to their redemption. By the time Miner entered its gates, San Quentin had grown into a complex of three triple-story buildings crammed with tiny cells a little more than a three feet wide and less than ten feet long. Two men shared each cell. Every day, between 5 and 7 a.m., depending on the season, the men were roused by a bell and given 10 minutes to dress in their woolen striped prison garb. For a half-hour they were allowed to walk the grounds before eating a 15-minute breakfast in complete silence. They then filed, one hand clamped to the shoulder of the man in front of them, to their assigned jobs until 11:30 a.m. when a meagre lunch was rapidly served and eaten. Then it was back to work until 4:30 p.m., when they broke for a 15-minute supper. Free time followed in their locked cells, with barely enough room to stretch their arms. Then, at 9 p.m. the prison was blacked out. The same soul-robbing routine went on day after day.

A more than 16-foot-high wall separated the 700 prisoners on San Quentin's 6 acres from the rest of the world. Guards armed with grapeshot cannon continually surveyed the prison yard from watchtowers and patrolled the walls. They circled the perimeter on horseback and wandered among the men with canes, on a constant lookout for trouble. Misbehaving prisoners were punished without compassion. As many as 10 a day were publicly whipped with rubber truncheons or forced to stand tip-toe for hours on a circle barely 8 inches in diameter. If they collapsed, they were beaten again.

They were flogged for "dumb insolence," an ill-defined crime. For something as serious as a surly glance, they might be sent to the "hooks," an area of the prison yard where their hands were bound behind them and then slowly pulled upward until they passed out from pain. If the "hooks" didn't adjust a prisoner's attitude, he might be given the "water cure," a punishment where high-pressure hoses doused him to the point of drowning. In particularly grievous circumstances, punishment for attempted escape, for example, the man might be banished to solitary confinement in "the hole."

The hole was a black tunnel beneath the prison only about 49 feet long. Seven small caves in the tunnel stonewall formed cells with an iron grate for a door. The only entrance to this dungeon was a hand-forged iron barricade. There were no lights in the hole, no beds, no ventilation. Prisoners, sometimes three or four to a cell, slept on the damp floor cushioned only by a blanket, if they were lucky. Meals of bread and water were served on the whim of the guards and if the prisoners complained, the guards had a simple, effective punishment. Lime would be scattered on the cell floor and then wet down. The guards would patiently wait for their caustic soup, with its oxygen-robbing fumes and skin-searing touch, to change the shouts of complaint to whimpers of despair.

There was an even darker side to the prison that, as young men, Miner and Sinclair may not have been prepared to endure. With violent men, separated for long periods from access to women, homosexuality was a fact of life at San Quentin. Brutal rape and sexual abuse were rampant, especially in the jute mill, blessed as it was by dark, isolated corners and convenient bales of burlap. One chronicler of San Quentin history reported that sexual abuse often struck more fear in younger prisoners than all the warden's other disciplinary measures. The young men were easy pickings for aggressive homosexuals. Bill, who was slightly built and only 19, was undoubtedly a target for the sexual predators.

Once admitted to the "family" at San Quentin, most prisoners were assigned a work detail. The penitentiary had a brickyard, a blacksmith shop, a leather works, and a jute mill, all of which were operated to generate income for the facility. The jute mill was infamous as a "tryst palace."

After a month in San Quentin, Bill Miner pleaded guilty to the Newcastle horse theft and was sentenced to an additional year. That autumn his mother began a heartfelt mission to extract a pardon from the California governor for her young son. But even with the support she solicited from sympathetic police, her requests went unheard. It wasn't until July 12, 1870, that Bill was released. He'd accumulated enough "coppers" (time credits for good behavior) to gain early freedom as a reformed criminal. At 23 years of age, and after three years in San Quentin, Bill was indeed a changed man. But he certainly hadn't been reformed.

Chapter 2
Robbing Stagecoaches and Dressing Fancy

an Quentin provided a few benefits for Bill Miner. Prison forced him to confront his own sexuality. Although there was plenty of evidence that he enjoyed the companionship of willing females, Bill developed an equal penchant for liaisons with men. San Quentin also gave him easy access to career tutoring.

As an inmate in California's notorious prison, Bill met the worst of a bad lot. In the least, he sharpened his ability to manipulate others to a fine edge. After six months toeing the line on the "outside," he joined forces with another convict he'd known from the prison yard. James "Alkali Jim" Harrington was a three-timer in San Quentin, convicted for burglary and stage robbery in and around the San Francisco area. The 26-year-old bandit evidently agreed to share his job experience with his protégé Bill Miner and another San Quentin alumnus named Charlie Cooper (also known as George Robertson).

Cooper had gotten out of prison the previous October and secured himself a job with the Stockton–Copperopolis Railroad, setting rails. While he worked, he acquired knowledge of the territory around the mining town of Angels Camp. On January 23, 1871, armed with weapons they'd stolen from a dry goods store in Stockton, the trio made their way to a secluded spot on the Sisson & Company San Andreas-to-Stockton stagecoach route and there waited to ambush the stage. At five o'clock that morning as the stagecoach slowed for a creek crossing, Miner stepped out of the bushes and waved his arms. It wasn't unusual to have travelers want to board the stage in isolated country, so the driver invited Miner to climb aboard. Bill had to unbuckle the straps on the stage to gain access, but he fumbled with the task. While the driver watched his "all thumbs" passenger, Alkali Jim and Charlie Cooper took positions in front of the stagecoach team and trained their shotguns on the driver. When the driver noticed the sudden change in circumstances, he shook his head. "There's no passengers," he told them tiredly.

Miner drew his pistol and tugged a hatchet from his belt. "It's the Wells Fargo's money chest we're after," he said. "Would you kindly toss it down?" The driver complied and began to urge his horses forward, but Miner told him to wait as he unsuccessfully hacked at the chest. Frustrated at being unable to open it, he peeked into the coach and noticed a mailbag.

"I guess we'll have that too," he said.

"I don't see what you want with that bag, there is none but letters in there."

Miner frowned, now getting angry. He asked about a bag stuffed under the driver's seat and was told it contained only ropes and straps.

"Are there any boots on board?"

"Just the ones I got on."

"Haul them off then," Miner ordered. "One of my boys out here wants a pair of boots."

The driver protested that he would have to steer the stagecoach barefoot, but it had no effect on Miner. Alkali Jim took off his old boots and tossed them to the driver.

"I don't want to put on these. I'd rather go without them. They'll dirty my stockings." Miner forced the driver at gunpoint to don Alkali Jim's dirty boots, but since Jim couldn't fit the driver's pair, they switched back again. By this time Bill's frustration was showing. Angrily, he asked if the driver had any money. With reluctance the driver said yes and passed over $5.50. "I won't have money to go on for the rest of my journey."

"I can't help that," Miner answered. He then also asked for the driver's watch.

"Look here boys, take my coat, take anything, but I don't want you to take my watch. It was a present to me." He told the bandits it was a gift from his mother. The robbers finally conceded that their heist was a pitiful failure and agreed to allow the driver to leave with his mother's gift.

When the stagecoach was out of sight, Bill and Jim carried the Wells Fargo chest away from the creek. After slashing at the padlock for several minutes, Jim managed to break the hasp with Bill's hatchet. They found $200 in gold coins and another $2400 worth of gold dust inside the box. The robbery had not been a complete waste of time after all.

Hastily the men covered the distance between the robbery site and the town of Jackson where they stumbled across an old prospector's cabin. Upon breaking in, Alkali Jim was delighted to find a pair of boots that fit. After changing and leaving his decrepit pair in their place, he tossed their shotguns into a creek and the trio continued on to the town of Ione Valley. They reached it after dark. Afraid of being spotted with the loot from the stagecoach robbery, they decided to hide it under a shed, taking with them just enough to pay for a hotel room.

Miner celebrated that night, confident that his tiny gang had gotten away with their crime. He regaled his partners with colorful descriptions of how he intended to squander his money in San Francisco and make up for all his penniless years in prison. Harrington added an invitation to visit his old robbing grounds in San Jose. Early the next morning they retrieved their hoard and, still on foot, traveled to Brighton where they were able to hop a freight train toward Stockton. Before reaching town they jumped off and separated. Miner went into town alone while Harrington and Cooper trudged in from a different direction. Their plan was to head for the train depot where they could make good their escape.

On his way through Stockton, Miner took a detour. At one of the best stores in town, he splurged on a new $23 suit. It was an outrageous act. Miner had been dressed as a common farm hand. Just entering the store was grounds for a few long looks. Worse, the price he paid was as much as a month's wages. The store clerks must have had questions about where an itinerant laborer might get that kind of money, in gold no less. The risk didn't even cross Bill's mind. He wanted to dress fancy for San Francisco just as he had in his youth, and that was all that mattered to him at that moment.

Using Bill's shopping as an excuse, Alkali Jim left Cooper at the depot and said he too needed to buy a shirt. Instead, Jim used the chance to cheat Cooper out of his share of the loot. Jim found a spot to hide the gold under a sidewalk and then returned to the depot and said he'd barely managed to avoid being recognized by two San Francisco policemen. Jim gave Cooper a handful of coins and asked him to buy the shirt. The second Cooper left, Jim retrieved the gold. Then he and Bill boarded a train bound for Frisco.

When Cooper got back to the depot a short while later, he discovered his cohorts had vanished. At first he suspected the police might have forced his partners to flee. He searched every saloon in Stockton and then wandered the outskirts of town before finally realizing he'd been double-crossed. Cooper bought himself a ticket to San Francisco, but had no luck finding them there either. Because they'd planned to hide in San Jose after celebrating in San Francisco, Cooper then headed south. After days of searching, however, he gave up and returned to San Francisco with a plan to watch the bordellos until his ex-partners appeared. Cooper hadn't figured on the stagecoach driver's careful description of his robbers, however, and before he could settle himself he was arrested. With no more than a new shirt to show for his criminal effort, Cooper was eager to get revenge. He confessed to the stage robbery and implicated Bill Miner and Jim Harrington.

Cooper's guess as to their whereabouts had been accurate. In fact, while he was searching the bordellos, Miner had attempted a clothes-buying shopping spree with some of the gold dust. Miner had been stymied when a store clerk refused to take gold dust as payment unless it was first weighed by Wells, Fargo & Company. That had spooked Bill and Alkali Jim enough to leave town. Again, Cooper hadn't been far off on his guesses because they did head for San Jose as planned.

Bill and Jim didn't realize that their descriptions had been provided to police departments across California. The two jailbirds thought they could blend in on the streets of San Jose, but their blending left a lot to be desired. At six o'clock on a foggy January 27 morning, a policeman noticed Miner and Harrington lurking in an otherwise deserted area near the train depot. He ordered them to identify themselves.

Alkali Jim pulled a derringer from his pocket and Bill drew his revolver. The policeman, realizing he was about to be shot, fumbled with his own holster. Somehow his gun belt had slipped from under his arm to his back. As he awkwardly tugged on the leather straps, Alkali Jim fired, but all he heard was a dull snap. The percussion cap had exploded on the derringer's bullet. The delay gave the policeman just enough time to find his gun and fire two shots. Harrington quickly retreated into the fog, leaving Miner to dodge for cover where he too tried to fire, but in his case not even the cap exploded. The policeman didn't realize how close Bill Miner had been to killing him and he dashed into the fog after Jim.

The two bandits should have suspected that the policeman might file a report with the San Francisco authorities. They would have been better off had they attempted to escape in another direction. Instead, Bill and Jim took the first train back to the big city. They needed to liquidate their stolen loot, so the two weighed the gold dust into three bags using a grocer's scale and then traded it with a broker for gold coins. Alkali Jim said he had a woman friend in Mayfield who would hide them until the heat was off, but Bill declined the invitation, thinking he could hide more easily in the port city. That decision granted him a few extra days of freedom.

Using information supplied by Cooper, the police

pounced on Alkali Jim in Mayfield. With a good description of Bill willingly provided by Cooper, police fanned out in the city. Two detectives spotted Bill Miner on February 5, 1871, as he casually strolled along a San Francisco street with bundles of new clothes in his arms. They apprehended him without a fight.

Cooper was released because of his help, but Bill and Jim were taken to the San Andreas jail and locked in chains. During the next month the men attempted to escape twice, once by filing through their chains with a case knife and another time by using the wire handle on a water bucket. The attempts only riled their captors. On June 6, 1871, still draped in 45 pounds of chain, the men were sentenced to 10 years each in San Quentin. Miner had managed to remain free from jail for just one year.

Their stay in the prison looked as though it might be brief, however. G.W. Tyler, their defense attorney, appealed their sentence to the California Supreme Court. Tyler claimed that, because they were forced to stand trial in chains, the jury had been unfairly prejudiced against them.

The justices had to agree. On March 18, 1872, the pair was brought to trial again. During a body search at the courthouse lock-up, both were found to be hiding escape devices. Miner had a saw blade in the sole of his boot and Harrington had one in the waistband of his trousers. Their new judge, already angered at having to deal with the obviously guilty pair, was not amused by their antics. He gave them only a brief review of previous evidence and then promptly boosted their sentences to 13 years in San Quentin, without credit for time already served.

It was a blow to Miner and it turned him into a desperately furtive convict who became obsessed with escape. On May 7, 1874 he staged a fight with another inmate, but was caught and rewarded with 20 lashes and nine days in the dungeon. The other prisoner had apparently concocted the escape scheme and then given the prison guards a tip-off to advance his own case for clemency. When Bill realized he was unable to trust either his cellmates or his guards, he finally understood that the penal system formed more than just a phalanx of high walls around him. Bill began to realize that if he wanted to get out, he had to fight the system. Between August 1874 and February 1880, Bill wrote 11 letters to authorities pleading for a commutation of his sentence. His *communiqués* were literate and eloquent. He used the unfair appeal judgment, his good behavior, and even his mother's declining health as reasons for mercy. Bill stated that he'd learned the trade of shoemaking in prison and he promised to leave California forever, move to Colorado to live with his sister, and become a law-abiding citizen.

His sister Mary Jane had married a mining man with interests near Leadville, Colorado, and she promised that Bill would be given a job as an alternative occupation if he were released early. She verified that her mother's health was poor, adding that the tragic death of Bill's young brother

Ben had left her mother without any male support in her old age. The facts were all true. Ben's death had been tragic. Ben had worked for a short time as a telegraph operator and had slipped into a spiral of depression because of a gambling addiction. He'd threatened suicide on several occasions and on June 15, 1871 he carried out his final threat by shooting himself in the head.

However, the barrage of pleas didn't soften the California governor's heart. Despite Bill's claims, the record showed he was far from being a model prisoner. He had altercations with other prisoners and one in particular had fermented into a feud. On August 10, 1879, Bill had sneaked into another convict's cell with a prison chum, and beaten the man brutally. For the deed, Bill was given 20 lashes and the blemish on his behavior record was glaring. Bill had to serve his time, the governor said, pure and simple. But eventually his extended stay at San Quentin worked in his favor. After he helped fight a fire that threatened to destroy the jute mill, all his credits, including the ones taken from him before the second sentence, were restored. When Bill had served nine years, he was released. On July 14, 1880, at the age of 33, he once again turned his back on the gates of San Quentin.

Chapter 3
A Nasty Protégé
and a Lynching

ill Miner was a creature of habit. Once he was out of prison, he made a brief attempt at being a law-abiding citizen. He visited his sister, relaxing and acclimatizing himself to freedom. Settlers in the territory around Leadville, Colorado, played loose with the law, which was a tempting environment for the old jailbird. Leadville was a booming community of 15,000 inhabitants in the 1880s. It had attracted a mix of eager entrepreneurs, flim-flam artists, and shady characters along with hard-working miners and farmers. The famous and the infamous could be counted among the residents, including characters like Doc Holiday, Calamity Jane, Wild Bill Hickock, and Soapy Smith.

In mid-September, four weeks after arriving in Colorado,

Bill decided to see Denver. On the southbound train he was attracted to a young man who appeared to have a lust for adventure. Twenty-three-year-old Iowa farming boy, Arthur Pond, was on his way to Silver Cliff and a job with the railroad. Bill, as a gentlemanly fellow traveler with soft speech and a friendly manner, managed to discourage the impetuous youth from those plans before they reached the Mile High City. He introduced himself as "California Bill" and, probably embellishing on his criminal career, impressed upon Pond that there were much easier ways to earn a living in mining country than swinging a pick for the railroad. By the time their train reached Canon City and they stepped off, Pond was ready to test Miner's claims. Maybe Bill thought he'd found a willing lover and a gullible sidekick, but the boy was far from being either.

Pond adopted a criminal mindset almost too easily. He immediately created the alias Billy LeRoy and began to carry himself with a threatening swagger. He was the opposite of the gentle, unassuming Bill Miner. Since neither of the men had much in the way of resources, they decided to work in Canon City as laborers to "get the lay of things." They soon earned enough of a stake to buy the tools of their trade — six-shooters. LeRoy had worked in Pitkin and he knew the Barlow–Sanderson Stagecoach that traveled through the area often carried bullion. Miner thought that would be the perfect setting for Pond's introduction to crime, especially considering that by the time they'd walked over Marshall's

Pass and made their ambush camp about 6 miles outside of Pitkin, they had only 25 cents to share between them.

Miner waited patiently at the ambush site for a whole day, while LeRoy described just how much gold would be on the stage. It must have seemed a dream come true. In a few hours Miner would be back in the pink. To his dismay, however, at 10 p.m. on September 23, it wasn't a stagecoach that came bouncing toward them on the rutted trail. Since LeRoy had last been in Pitkin, the Barlow-Sanderson stage line had changed its route and was now only dispatching a buckboard from Pitkin to connect with the stagecoach at Buena Vista. Miner, hungry and broke, decided they should rob it anyway.

Waving his revolver with menace for LeRoy's educational benefit, and with gruff authority, Miner ordered the driver to pass him the treasure box. There wasn't one. Miner countered with another demand for the express box, instead. There wasn't one of those, either. "Well then pass the mailbags," Miner ordered. The driver did as he was told, then gladly accepted Miner's invitation to carry on. Bill allowed LeRoy the honor of picking through the first of the two sacks right on the trail, but finding nothing of value he led his new partner out of sight to examine the second. Disgruntled, Bill shared half of the proceeds of his first robbery in 10 years — the grand sum of $50.

The experienced thief had already had enough of his novice partner's "insider knowledge" and insisted they travel back to Canon City the way they'd come. Moving only by night to avoid detection, Miner promptly got lost. It took several days without food before they reached Lake City and once they'd found a restaurant and hotel, it only took a few days to eat and drink through their cash. Bill was too tired for a distant tramp on foot to another hold-up. On October 7 he opted to guide Billy LeRoy to Slumgullion Pass, only 5 miles from Lake City, and there he ordered Billy to hold up the stage when it passed. Then, while LeRoy covered him with a rifle, Miner relieved the stage of four mail sacks. In his haste he overlooked the registered mail, which usually contained cash or valuables, so one more time their haul was almost worthless at only $100. Miner must have felt the sting of embarrassment. He convinced LeRoy to help him rob the Barlow–Sanderson Stagecoach one last time in the San Luis Valley. To avoid the possibility of being arrested for their $100 faux pas, Miner led LeRoy southward using the mountainside timber as cover. Again, he lost his way. The men wandered in circles for two days without food or water. Only by luck on October 10, just as a blizzard was beginning, did they stumble upon the tiny hamlet of Wagon Wheel Gap. Though he was near freezing, exhausted, and half-starved, Miner wasn't going to take the chance of being arrested for a measly $100 trick. He stayed within the cloak of the timbers and heavy snowfall and sent LeRoy into the village to buy meat and bread.

The two men ate and slept for two days in an improvised shelter outside Wagon Wheel Gap before resuming their trek to Del Norte where Bill was certain he'd finally locate a stagecoach ripe for plucking. It took them until October 14 to reach a suitable ambush point. By then, LeRoy was fed up with his mentor. Nothing so far had resembled Miner's description of an easy job. California Bill must have appeared to be a tired old failure. LeRoy decided to take matters into his own hands this time around.

The Del Norte stage route followed the Rio Grande to South Fork where it turned to Creede, Colorado. From there the trail wound its way for more than 55 miles through the mountains and finally crossed the Continental Divide at Slumgullion Pass.

At three o'clock in the morning the stage rumbled toward the two men on its way to Lake City. LeRoy stepped out of the bush ahead of Bill and took charge of the operation. He ordered Bill to guard the driver and hold the horses while he rifled through the coach searching for booty. When LeRoy withdrew four mail sacks and a registered-mail pouch, he curtly ordered Miner to release the horses and tell the driver to get moving. That wasn't Bill's style. He slowly moved out of the way of the team, and tugged the brim of his floppy hat. "Sorry for the 10 minute delay," Miner said to the driver. "Take care on the road." All the victims of the robbery would remember the older bandit's courtesy and his young confederate's brash menace.

Though LeRoy's tactics had embarrassed Bill, he couldn't complain about the results because they were much better than either had hoped. The registered-mail pouch held $3600 in gold dust and coin.

In the early morning darkness, LeRoy quickly split the spoils. As the sun would be rising soon, Miner suggested they flee before daylight. A posse would quickly be dispatched to find them because of the size of the haul, but LeRoy flatly refused. There'd be no more night time running from posses that never came, no more getting lost in the mountains, he told the older man. LeRoy insisted on returning to their ambush camp and sleeping until daylight. Not wanting to travel alone, Miner reluctantly agreed, and through the night stood guard over his drowsing partner. The decision to stay was a poor one. The few hours of relaxation were just enough for Armstrong, the hard-riding sheriff of Rio Grande, to mount up and start his chase, just as Bill had predicted. On foot, the robbers were no match for Armstrong's horse. He easily tracked them to Spring Creek Pass as they trudged their way to Fort Garland the next morning. At one point in the pursuit, the sheriff was close enough to fire his gun at the men, but Miner's luck was holding. Sheriff Armstrong lost their trail and headed off at a gallop in the wrong direction. Bill insisted on hiding until dark and LeRoy finally agreed.

The two reached Fort Garland the next morning just in time to board a train to Pueblo. Finally relaxing a little, Bill ended their relationship the way it began, on a train. He told LeRoy he'd already taught him everything he knew about robbery, including how to pick handcuffs. He had only a final piece of advice to offer. Get out of the state. LeRoy responded with ridicule. He reminded the ex-con about all the mistakes he'd made in their short partnership. He confidently told California Bill to mind his own business.

Miner was probably relieved to be separated from his protégé, considering LeRoy's aggressive style and the embarrassing fact that the robbery LeRoy engineered was the only one they'd committed that was worthwhile.

As it turned out, LeRoy might have done better for himself had he taken Bill's advice. Instead of fleeing quietly, LeRoy decided to team with his brother Silas and another man named Frank Clark to rob another stage near Del Norte. Their haul in the San Luis Valley robbery was enormous at $15,000, and large enough to merit a posse of trained trackers. Clark managed to elude capture but LeRoy and his brother were traced to Kansas City and arrested. A U.S. marshal escorted the men on a train to Del Norte where they were to be held for trial, but en route LeRoy remembered one of Bill's lessons. In the train lavatory he dismantled his pocket watch and using the mainspring, picked the lock on his handcuffs. In a dash for freedom, he climbed through the lavatory window and dropped from the moving train. However, his attempted escape was noticed by the observant marshal. The train was stopped and a limping LeRoy was easily recaptured. Things only got worse for Leroy and his brother after that. In the Del Norte jail they were easy targets for a mob of miners who were tired of being victims of stagecoach bandits. A group of them stormed the jail — seized the men — and lynched them. It was a dramatic example for anyone who contemplated holding up a stage at Del Norte.

Had Miner stuck it out with LeRoy, he may have come to the same ignoble end. Instead, the wily bandit was flush and forgotten. It was the first time in his career Bill had executed a rich heist and not been caught. He hopped a train for Chicago and in the Windy City celebrated with visits to the bordellos and saloons. Then he bought himself a full wardrobe of new clothes in the latest fashion and contemplated his next move. He needed a safe haven for a few months and being so close to it, decided his hometown of Onondaga, Michigan, would be a perfect spot to rest and recuperate.

Chapter 4
A Tattooed Gentleman

round Christmas 1880, Bill Miner returned to Vevay Township, a place he hadn't seen since he was 10 years old. He had two Saratoga trunks crammed with fine clothes, a fabricated story to explain his wealth, and a new name to match — William A. Morgan.

Bill seemed the epitome of cultured upbringing and prosperity. A lush drooping moustache handsomely framed his square chin. His keen blue eyes sparkled with easy and untroubled delight as he kidded, dazzled, and deceived the residents of Onondaga into believing he was a rich mining man from California. He had the clothes, the manners, and the money to back up his façade. Bill decided that Onondaga, the place he was born, would become his bolthole after the occasional sojourn into the western territories for a little stagecoach mayhem. In Onondaga, if he set the scene properly, no one would ever think of questioning him about where his wealth came from. It would be a place where he could spend freely and never work, just as life would have been, if his father had not met such an untimely end.

Everything was fine except for the India ink tattoos that peppered his body. While in San Quentin, Bill had acquired additional marks. He now had a tattoo of a ballet dancer on his right forearm, another at the base of his left thumb, and a heart pierced with a dagger and two stars on his left arm. Still, Bill gave the impression that he was a fine gentleman. He ingratiated himself with the community's leading citizens and it wasn't long before he had a doting cadre of friends. In a very private joke, he explained to anyone who asked that he was in the Onondaga area to settle an estate and that he was the only surviving heir. He told people that he also owned property in Sacramento, buildings in San Francisco, and mines in California and Mexico. The eligible bachelor's obvious wealth attracted the attention of Onondaga's debutantes as well, among them the daughter of Henry Willis, a prosperous and respected businessman and officer of the township.

Jennie Louise Willis was 21 years old and anxious to find a husband. Bill happily encouraged the attractive young woman's attentions. He squired her about on rides in the countryside. He escorted her to Onondaga's finest restaurants and lavishly treated her to expensive gifts. Within weeks

Jennie confessed to having fallen in love with the dashing older man, and Bill proposed marriage. He may have had an ulterior motive in making the proposal. After three months of wild spending, Bill's stockpile of gold had almost vanished. Marriage to the daughter of the wealthy Onondaga township officer might have resulted in a sizeable dowry. On the other hand, it could have been a stall as Bill tried to figure out a way to sever himself from Onondaga without ruining the myth he'd created.

Bill solved his problem by telling his new friends that he had to return to California to deal with his aged mother's health. "She needs to take an extended ocean voyage to restore her vitality," he told them, and the honest folk of Onondaga believed him. While Jennie was heartbroken over the temporary separation, Bill's future father-in-law commended him for his duty to his mother. He threw the dapper con a farewell banquet that was attended by the town's most prominent citizens. In naïve faith, Jennie continued to build her *trousseau*, even purchasing an expensive bridal gown. Bill, of course, intended to break every promise he'd ever made to her.

Years later, he confessed to a reporter that his cruel deception had never bothered his conscience at all. "Of course it was all hot air. If I had saved that money, I might be right there now, the head of a happy family. Oh, but it was great fun."

Before leaving Michigan, Bill befriended an itinerant

49

laborer named Stanton T. Jones and let him in on his secret identity. Jones had witnessed Bill's fast-spending habits and he took the fancy clothes that William A. Morgan always wore as proof there was money to be made with a revolver in Colorado. Bill and his new partner arrived in Denver sometime in January 1881. To get seed money for his next operation, Bill sold his trunks and clothes, and replaced them with used attire, six-shooters, and a Winchester rifle. With barely enough cash between them to purchase stagecoach tickets, the two men headed south, back to Del Norte and the bullion. True to his prison-engendered nature, Bill also befriended a tall gangly boy of 19 years as another accomplice.

Charles B. Dingman's effeminate appearance may have appealed to Bill. The six-foot youth, with his sandy hair and blue eyes, knew what life in prison was like. But perhaps he was a good gang recruit for reasons other than campfire companionship. He'd served time in the Colorado State Penitentiary five years earlier for cattle theft and afterward he had worked as a stock tender for the Barlow–Sanderson Stagecoach Company. As a result, the "Swede," as he was known, was very familiar with his employer's schedule for gold shipments.

The men followed the bank of the Rio Grande in the direction of South Fork on foot, until Bill found a likely hold-up spot. Just after midnight on February 4, 1881, Charles was given the job of holding the team of stagecoach horses while Bill and Stanton committed the gang's first robbery. Thugs hadn't stopped the Barlow–Sanderson stage in four months, likely because of the lynching example the Del Norte towns- folk had made of Miner's previous partner and his brother. Bill, of course, was unaware of the hanging but he knew how effective the tenacious Rio Grande sheriff was as a tracker of criminals in the Colorado Mountains.

Miner stopped the stage and issued his now patented command of "Hands up!" to the driver and the four pas- sengers. He apologized for causing a delay in their journey, efficiently relieved the stagecoach of its mailbag cargo, and sent it on its way. The trail dust hadn't even settled before the men tore through the bags looking for loot. But Bill found nothing worth value. Dingman had picked the wrong stage to rob and Bill was livid. Bill demanded an explanation from Charles. Dingman suggested that per- haps the company had secretly altered the schedules after the lynching.

"What lynching?" Bill inquired.

"Guy named LeRoy and his brother got strung up a few months back," Dingman explained.

Bill was suddenly alert. "Didn't get caught by a lawman named Armstrong by any chance?"

Dingman nodded. "He tracked them all the way to Kansas."

Bill exploded with rage. "We're in a tight spot now then!" he shouted with uncharacteristic temper. "That bull's got a second sight when it comes to tracking. You're on your own and I hope you got luck in your pocket!" Bill tugged Stanton away. "We need horses or we're goners," he said with rueful seriousness. "While it's still dark, we can borrow some from the ranch we saw a ways back."

The men left Charles Dingman to engineer his own escape. He didn't try to follow them and wasn't worried because he was sure none of the Del Norte stage passengers had recognized him. He was wrong. A bounty was placed on the three bandits and a police hunt was mounted for the stock handler immediately. Within two weeks, Charles was resting uncomfortably in the Alamosa City Jail, pleading he'd been led astray by an older man named Morgan and claiming his role in the robbery was minimal. Despite the fact he didn't carry a weapon in the robbery and only held the horses, he was sentenced to 10 years at hard labor in the federal prison in Wyoming. The description he gave of his partners was poor, and perhaps even misleading, because Bill and Stanton were able to beat their way to Leadville on their stolen horses without a problem.

With Miner's brother-in-law's help, Bill and Stanton got mining jobs near Leadville and for several months avoided any notice. By mid-April, however, Bill was ready to try again.

While in Leadville, he made the acquaintance of another young man to replace his last recruit. James East, a 23-year-old farm boy who'd come to Colorado from Illinois, was an easy target for Bill's greasy persuasion. The trio left Leadville on foot and surfaced again in Saguache County, on April 18, where they stole three horses. Mistakenly thinking they got away clean, the men were followed by one of the ranchers they'd relieved of stock. In the meantime, a posse was formed by Sheriff Armstrong to capture them. Bill and his confederates managed to avoid the sheriff in the mountains one more time, but in Wagon Wheel Gap an alert tollkeeper noticed the men suspiciously moving through town in the dead of night and reported their direction. By dawn the next day the tired riders were captured.

Accounts of what happened next differ in exact details, but what is known is that the men were bound with hay-baling wire and the sheriff decided to camp overnight before taking his prisoners to Del Norte. During the night, Bill managed to untie himself. The sheriff noticed in time to reach for his rifle, but not fast enough. With a .32 caliber pistol that had been hidden in his boot, Bill defended himself. He fired four shots. The first broke the arm of the deputy sheriff on guard, and the second fractured Armstrong's right arm, as well.

For months after, the two bandits continued to evade detection and recapture as they skittered from bolthole to bolthole in Colorado. Bill may have been more cautious than usual, considering the fact that he was now wanted for stagecoach robbery as well as the attempted murder of a lawman. In late summer, he and Stanton emerged from hiding in California. He had no crimes hanging over him there, but to be safe he invented a new alias — William Anderson — to help confuse any would-be pursuers.

Chapter 5
Back in the Hole

ill had taken ill when he and Stanton surfaced at Chinese Camp in Tuolumne County, California, in October 1881. Suffering from a high fever and chills, Bill's condition was apparently so severe that he was near death. Stanton had nursed him in the small mining camp for weeks. During his slow recovery, Bill took the opportunity to meet his neighbors. In his relaxed state, complemented by his charming nature, he easily and naturally found new friends. While socializing, Bill came across James Crum, a San Quentin crony. Crum introduced him to William A. Miller, a slow-witted ex-con who owned a small spread outside Woodland that was reputed to be a hangout for wanted men. Crum, a man with a blood-chilling gaze and a thick Colonel Saunders-

type goatee, had been a notorious Pacific Coast horse thief and stage robber. Miller, a seething sort, had been incarcerated for robbery and assault. The two men told Miner that gold was regularly shipped to Sonora from the mining town of Angels Camp. Thus, Bill used his month of recovery in Chinese Camp to plan the new gang's first team robbery.

Traveling to Angels Camp on November 6, under the ruse of attending a country-dance, the men prepared for their heist. That evening, Bill, an ever-ready flirt, spotted an attractive singer and introduced himself as William A. Anderson. He spent the entire dance with her, plying his charms. When she indicated she was having trouble locating sheet music in her rustic surroundings, Bill politely suggested he might be of service. He told the girl he was planning a trip in the immediate future and would be pleased to locate some sheet music as a special favor.

The following day, the gang went to work executing Bill's plan to rob the Sonora-to-Milton stagecoach. It was a silent heist, because Bill orchestrated the men using only hand signals. One took charge of the team, another covered the driver with a rifle, and the third pulled the three passengers from the coach and had them line up with their hands in the air. It was plain to see who was leading the team. The driver asked Bill if there was anything of his the bandit may want.

"No, the drivers of this line are all damned fine fellows, and I would rather give them something than take anything from them," Bill replied. After some alarmed looks from his confederates, however, the polite robber had a change of mind. "I guess I'll search you; you may have a revolver and might get mad and try to use it."

As the driver was unarmed, Bill moved him away from the coach and turned his full attention to the Wells Fargo & Company express shipment. The two ironbound chests and a safe presented only a minor challenge. On an earlier robbery, he'd used a hatchet to break the lock on the Wells Fargo strongbox. This time he replaced his "muscle-key" with a sledgehammer. The chests easily opened to expose $3300 in coin and gold dust. At the same time, his gang members searched the passengers and coach and discovered another $550 stuffed in a gunnysack. The second find boosted the bandits' curiosity and they began meticulously searching everything.

"Hurry up. I don't want to miss the train at Milton!" the driver barked impatiently.

Courteous as ever, Bill acquiesced. He shook the driver's hand and thanked the passengers for their co-operation. With a jocular "ta-ta, my boy," he waved to the driver as the gang disappeared into the woods.

The California law fraternity reacted with tremendous speed in an attempt to apprehend this gang of silent robbers and their gentleman leader before they could flee too far. The manhunt that was mounted became one of northern California's broadest. From a wide surrounding area, 18 sheriffs, deputies, constables, and detectives scoured the countryside for evidence to show where the bandits may have gone. The chief investigator for Wells Fargo & Company, Detective L. Aull, called the Pinkerton's National Detective Agency to the scene. The Pinkerton's detective, with the resources of his agency behind him, said the polite mannerisms of the bandit had all the earmarks of Bill Miner.

Using Miner's description, he asked questions and tracked his suspect to the Angels Camp dance. There he learned about the charming man who the singer identified as William A. Anderson. "That's Miner without a doubt," the Pinkerton's detective proclaimed. The girl told of how Anderson had promised to send her some sheet music. While the police combed the area for the robbers, the agency waited patiently for the mail to point the way to Miner's whereabouts.

After the robbery, Miller split with his share of the loot and returned to his small farm. Riding only at night, the remaining gang members made it unseen all the way to Oakland, and then to San Francisco five days later. With money to spend, Bill satisfied his penchant for fine clothing before doing anything else. He purchased a silk vest, an $85 suit, a double-breasted chinchilla coat, and then added a gold watch and chain to his ensemble. With a new pair of nickel-plated Smith & Wesson revolvers belted to his hips, he was once again the epitome of high fashion. Bill Miner gave every impression of being a man of wealth and breeding. He mailed his Angels Camp sweetheart the sheet music he'd promised and said good bye to Stanton Jones, who wanted to stay in the port city. With Crum, Miner rode back to Chinese Camp. Bill intended to collect a private reward from the grateful girl, but agreed to go with Crum to Miller's ranch for a visit first.

The law wasn't far behind them. Acting on leads uncovered in San Francisco, detectives arrived at the ranch and tried to surround it. Spotted by the desperados first, however, the detectives were hundreds of yards from their target when Miner, Crum, and Miller made a dash for their horses. Reacting quickly, the lawmen managed to block the bandits' run to freedom. Crum dived for cover with his shotgun, ready to hold off the posse while Miner and Miller tried to vanish into the brush.

It took the posse 15 minutes to subdue Crum before they could renew their pursuit of Miner and Miller. By that time the two had effectively vanished. Detective Aull and another officer named Arlington searched through the night and the following day in a futile attempt to pick up Miner's tracks. The lawmen were approximately 10 miles from Sacramento and were about to give up when they suddenly spotted the fugitives by the Sacramento River. Afraid to spook the bandits and possibly lose them again, Aull decided to try a bluff. He sent Arlington in a wide circle to guard against an escape along the bank in the opposite direction. Then he draped his shotgun over his arm and nonchalantly approached the fugitives. Miner and Miller drew their revolvers.

"Hold on there, boys!" Aull shouted, "I'm just out here to do some duck hunting."

Miner surveyed the visitor suspiciously and then smiled, holstering his revolver. "We thought you might be a highwayman. There are plenty of that sort around here."

The investigator stalled to give his partner enough time to get into position. "Not me. Just hunting ducks, but I got turned around and lost my party. Do you know the way to Stockton?" Miner helpfully offered directions and watched until Aull had disappeared from view, disregarding his intuition. He shouldn't have.

Suddenly, from a hidden position, Aull began to pepper the bandits' camp with shotgun pellets. With the blizzard of buckshot coming from two directions, Miller immediately surrendered, but Miner made a dash for freedom, running a zigzagging course away from the river. Arlington took charge of Miller and Aull took up the chase alone, repeatedly firing at Miner in an attempt to wound the bandit. After a mile-and-a-half foot race, with the detective gaining like a bloodhound, Miner finally surrendered in exhaustion.

Once the robbers were securely locked in the Sonora jail, the lawmen began an interrogation in an attempt to gain confessions. Miner and Miller refused to talk or implicate each other, but Crum was less loyal. Thinking he'd gain a lighter sentence, Crum confessed to the stagecoach robbery and named his partners. Faced with Crum's confession, the other two gave in. Luckily for Jones, he'd left California before the law could identify him. None of the others knew Stanton Jones' whereabouts.

On December 15, 1881, the trio was convicted for the stagecoach robbery. Because of their long records and the Pinkerton evidence against them, Miner and Miller were given maximum sentences of 25 years each in San Quentin. The judge was more lenient with Crum, perhaps because of his co-operation, sentencing him to only 12 years.

Crum managed to gain a pardon a couple of years later from Governor George Stoneman by grousing on some other former partners and testifying against them in a murder trial. For Miner, however, the sentence amounted to a life term and before long he was separated from Miller. In March 1882, Miller was transferred to Folsom Prison where Charles Aull, his captor, had become warden. From 1888 to 1895 Miller was a model prisoner. However, he was dying of tuberculosis. After four separate appeals for a compassionate discharge, he was finally granted a pardon in March 1897 and he died soon after his release.

As Prisoner 10191, Miner soon realized that not much had changed at San Quentin in the time he'd been gone. The 13 years already spent behind those walls gave him an old con's status in the penitentiary, and he revelled in his notoriety with the press. Otherwise, he served his time quietly without attracting the punishing attention of the guards or warden. In 1883, a reporter from the *New York Sun* interviewed Bill for a story on the Sonora stage robbery and wrote that he found Bill to be pleasant, friendly, and impressive. "He is now thirty-seven years of age and not withstanding his many years of confinement is yet a handsome and graceful fellow, fluent of tongue and captivating in style."

Warden Aull, however, knew better and he warned everyone that Bill Miner was not to be trusted. On April 17, 1884, Miner proved the warden correct. Bill had constructed a dummy and placed it in his bunk before hiding in a box in the prison yard. His plan had been to hide there until dark and then climb over the wall, but the guards weren't fooled by the crude stickman when they made their bed checks. Because of this attempted escape, the Prison Board fined Bill one night in the dungeon and revoked the credit time he'd amassed.

The old con artist didn't make another attempt to escape until November 29, 1892. Miner and his cellmate, Joe Marshall, used their job assignments to acquire a hefty list of escape materials. Bill was working as a leather cutter in the shoe shop and Marshall was in charge of the machine shop. Into their cell, over time, they managed to smuggle baling rope from the jute mill, a bent bar to fashion a grappling hook, a dark lantern to see with on a moonless night, and the parts they needed to assemble a ratchet drill. In the early morning hours, they drilled through the lock on their cell door and scurried to the stairway at the corner of their building with a plan to sneak past a guardhouse near the stairs. Marshall led the way. At the stairs he checked the empty prison yard and then confidently began to descend. In the space of a few steps — the blast of a shotgun from a blanket-covered window in the guards' quarters across the yard echoed on the prison walls — and a chunk of Marshall's skull disappeared. Miner collapsed to his knees in surrender, but a second blast pelted the wall above his head in response anyway. The blast missed its target but tore through his cheeks, shattering two of his teeth. He immediately lost consciousness.

Apparently, the guards had known about the escape plan for some time. They had posted men to wait for the attempt and their intent was to kill the escapees. But an inquiry later exonerated the guards and that seemed to drain Miner's will. For the next four years he was a model prisoner. When James Budd, the attorney who'd defended him 30 years before and promised to do anything in his power to help Miner, became California's governor, Miner reminded him of his promise. In four letters between 1897 and 1898 Bill pleaded for a pardon, promising to leave California and never return if Budd made good on his vow. Budd refused. It wasn't until June 17, 1901, after Bill had served nearly 20 years in prison, that the con once again tasted freedom.

At 54 years old, Miner had spent more than half his life behind bars. He'd served a total of 33 years and six months as a convict or in jail waiting for trials. Why he didn't just drift into obscurity after that horrid life is amazing. However, this was only the beginning of the creation of the myth of Billy Miner. The man's indefatigable character and his criminal history made him a cunning and formidable opponent of the law. His square face had been hardened by years of deprivation and self-discipline. He had learned how to manufacture a beguiling persona, one that disguised a simmering emotional storm behind a friendly smile. He'd honed an ability to evaluate weakness in others and then manipulate those failings to his advantage. He was, without a doubt, a new and dangerous version of the man who'd robbed the Sonora stage.

Chapter 6
New Country —
New Tricks

hen Bill Miner cleared the gates of San Quentin, the world had already begun a rapid adaptation to an escalating series of inventions and innovations that made the life of a bandit far more difficult. George Eastman had invented photographic film and the camera went into wide use, capturing current photos of desperados that could be employed in future identifications. Telephones helped spread alerts to interconnected police forces within minutes of a robbery. But the worst was the decision by Wells Fargo & Company to ship valuables on fast-moving trains instead of ponderous stagecoaches.

Bill's mother had passed away four months before his release. Though he had not corresponded with his family in two years, Bill traveled to Washington State where his sister,

Mary Jane, had moved during his incarceration. Once again, Bill adopted his William Morgan alias to avoid easy identification by law enforcement officials. During this time, he sought out an old San Quentin friend in the Bellingham–Sumas area. "Cowboy Jake" Terry, a counterfeiter and smuggler, and Bill Miner, the stagecoach bandit, had formed a strong bond of friendship.

Bill had made an effort to demonstrate his rehabilitation by working for two years at an oyster bed in Samish Bay. But during the summer of 1903 his attitude changed and his old habits began to return. First, he formed a close relationship with a 17-year-old boy in Whatcom County. Charles Hoehn had been orphaned at 12 and was living with friends at the Equality Colony, a co-operative living venture. The youth had suffered a minor run-in with the law, and had served a short time in the Mount Vernon jail for petty larceny.

Bill also renewed his criminal acquaintance with Gary Harshman, a habitual criminal living nearby in Oregon. At Harshman's coaxing, Bill agreed to return to his old robbing habits. Except that now, the target was going to be trains.

How fascinating it must have been for the young teen, Charles Hoehn, to meet the soft spoken gentleman with his tales of hardened criminals and the high times to be had living off crime. Bill promised to take the lad to Mexico, where the two would make easy money and live well, if Hoehn would participate in the "trick" that Harshman wanted to pull. Hoehn was easily sucked in by Bill's claim that the job was almost risk-free. Toward mid-August, Bill treated Charles to a trip to the circus in Portland, Oregon. There, he introduced Charles Hoehn to Gary Harshman as the third member of their new gang. The gang worked together in a lumber camp for a short while to raise the money they needed and to discuss the heist. When they felt they were ready, the trio took over an abandoned cabin on Government Island near Goble, Oregon, to make final preparations.

On September 19, the gang moved to the town of Clarnie, about 10 miles outside Portland, for the holdup. The job would be simple, Bill said. All they had to do was stop the train and then use a few sticks of dynamite to blow open the express car's safe. He sent Charles to the tracks with a set of red stop signals while he and Gary climbed a bank above the tracks from which they could jump onto the slowing train. Bill, however, hadn't done his homework very well. Charles waved the lantern at the approaching train, but as he was on the wrong side of the tracks the engineer ignored the signal to stop. As the train sped past, Bill and Gary argued. Bill wanted to light a few sticks of dynamite and toss them at the train in hopes of causing a derailment, but Harshman refused. Once the train rattled off into the distance, they had no other choice than to come up with a new plan.

Hoehn was sent to buy a boat in Goble and float it to Corbett, 21 miles from Portland. With the boat in place, Miner and Harshman then sent Hoehn to Corbett to wait for the Oregon Railway & Navigation Company, Fast Express

No. 6. Meanwhile, they walked to a train stop at Troutdale. When the train reached Troutdale, the two robbers climbed aboard and made their way over the tender to the engine. At gunpoint they ordered the engineer, Ollie Barrett, and the fireman, H.F. Stevenson, to stop the train at Corbett. "If you obey orders no harm will come to you, but if you attempt any trickery work, death will be your reward," the older bandit told the frightened railwaymen.

This time Miner's plan seemed to be working. When the train stopped, he ordered the two engineers off. Harshman shouted to Hoehn, calling him out of the shadows by name. The boy appeared at the end of the cars with a rifle and two long poles with sticks of dynamite dangling from the ends. Bill, obviously out of his depth when it came to the composition of the train, escorted the engineers to the baggage car — and not to the express car that held the safes. He shouted for the guards inside to open the door. When there was no reply, Bill cursed. His railway captives later said that Miner appeared extremely agitated.

"We'll blow it then!" Bill shouted. He took the sticks from Hoehn, put them against the door, and lit the fuses. The explosion did as Miner had hoped. It shattered the door. It was then he realized he'd selected the wrong car. The blast, and Bill's string of cuss words, attracted the attention of passengers. Hoehn forced them back with a few warning shots. As Miner pushed the engineer and fireman forward to the express car, Harshman ran ahead. Unfortunately, he ran right into a shotgun blast unleashed by the express messenger, F.A. Korner, who had suddenly realized he was being called on to defend his car. Harshman, in his unlucky position at the head of the line, took much of the blast in his head. Barrett, the engineer, had been shot in the shoulder. Miner had been hiding behind the fireman, using him as a shield, and he fired back. But he only succeeded in making Korner retreat to safety. Korner's attack had the exact affect he had hoped for. Seeing Harshman fall, Hoehn panicked and ran for the riverbank. Without an accomplice to cover his back, Miner also decided to flee, leaving Harshman bleeding on the track bed.

The robbery attempt was reported immediately and within a few hours a special train was dispatched to Corbett with a sheriff, a posse, and a superintendent from Pinkerton's National Detective Agency aboard. Gary Harshman was given medical aid and transferred in custody to a hospital in Portland. However, he refused to give his name and even refused to eat. While Harshman was being questioned, the posse scattered at the robbery site to find his partners. Miner and Hoehn had deserted Harshman immediately, however. They had rowed across the Columbia River to the Washington side and then split up with a plan to meet again in Tacoma.

Miner went back to work at the oyster bed and found a job for Hoehn at a shingle mill. Hoehn was now calling himself Charles Morgan. It seemed, at least for a while, that their crime would go unpunished, but the Pinkerton's detectives were not that willing to give up. With just a shred of a lead (the name "Hoehn," which Harshman had been overheard shouting during the robbery) the agency was able to locate a boy who said he knew Hoehn. Charles Hoehn, the boy told him, had taken his uncle's last name, Morgan, and was working in a mill near Tacoma.

Hopeful that Hoehn might lead him to the third robber, the Pinkerton's detective solicited his young informant's help. He got the lad a job working alongside Charles with the purpose of watching him and reporting any contact he had with older men.

On October 6, the Tacoma police identified their hospital guest as Gary Harshman and confronted him with their evidence. Harshman crumbled, telling the police his partners were Bill Morgan and his nephew Charles Morgan, and two more fictitious robbers no one had seen. With confirmation of Hoehn's involvement, the police arrested him the next day. After 48 hours of questioning, Charles Hoehn also confessed. He, too, claimed five men were involved and let it slip that Bill Miner was working in the oyster beds in Samish Bay. But Bill was wily enough not to count on loyalty after his bad experience with Crum 20 years earlier. By the first of October, Bill had already left his job on the coast and moved in with his sister in Whatcom. Thanks to the daily newspapers, Miner had probably learned of Harshman's confession and Hoehn's arrest, because on October 9 he disappeared, telling his sister he was going to Anacortes, Washington.

Bill left in such a hurry he forgot to take his blood-spattered overcoat with him. When a Portland sheriff arrived at Mary Jane's home with a warrant, the coat was discovered. Mary Jane said her brother was not Morgan but William A. Miner. She also told the sheriff her brother was going to Anacortes, but they either didn't understand what she meant or they ignored her report.

Pinkerton's National Detective Agency, on October 27, prepared a reward poster on a man they thought they knew well. Miner's physical description was given, including all his tattoos, and the agency identified another way Bill might be recognized. It stated, "[Miner] is said to be a [sodomite] and may have a boy with him." By November, even with a picture and the $1300 reward posted for him, Bill Miner was still a fugitive. In that same month Charles Hoehn and Gary Harshman were found guilty of the robbery and sentenced to prison.

While Pinkerton detectives and Oregon sheriffs searched for him in Washington, Miner called on the help of his old friend, smuggler Jake Terry, to help him cross into Canada. It's likely that Terry was familiar with little-known trails and that he guided Miner north, helping him reach the tiny ranching community of Princeton. The Nicola Valley just north of the border offered an inviting retreat to fugitives because the district was sparsely settled and lightly patrolled by lawmen. It was an area where a man was allowed his secrets and newcomers were taken at face value, no matter how outlandish their life stories seemed.

Bill took on another new name, George W. Edwards. George claimed he was a southern gentleman who'd come to Canada in search of a peaceful winter rest. Miner approached local rancher Bob Thornton, who took him to the Schisler family on Bald Mountain. Miner said he was willing to pay for accommodation over the winter and the cash-strapped farming family gratefully accepted his offer.

Over the winter months, Miner ingratiated himself with the Schislers and the townsfolk in Princeton. He helped flood a creek to make a skating rink for the Schisler's youngest daughter and entertained the Princeton ranching folk with avid fiddle playing at every social event. To everyone in the area, George Edwards was a kindly, polite, American cowboy and nothing more. Perhaps they considered his habit of always wearing his six-guns a bit odd, but no one feared the affectation in the least.

When spring arrived, Miner moved in with another local eccentric, an old rancher named Jack Budd who had a 360-acre spread 5 miles from Princeton. Budd was a gray-haired Texan of indeterminate age who'd originally come to British Columbia in the mid-1880s to prospect during the Granite Creek gold rush. When the rush petered out, he traded horses for a time north of Princeton before homesteading on Bald Mountain, close enough to the Schislers to be considered a neighbor.

Bill's near capture for the Portland robbery hadn't daunted his quest for easy money. He knew, from his time in

Onondaga, how gullible the residents of a community could be if he spent money freely. Bill related his "California gold mine" story to anyone willing to listen in the tiny British Columbia community. It explained his life of leisure and gave him ample opportunity to head to the coast "on business." During his many trips, Bill nurtured his partnership with his old San Quentin cellmate, Jake Terry. Terry was a man with a vicious temper and a keen criminal mind (in San Quentin he'd been nicknamed Terrible Terry). He'd spent time as a railroad engineer and had worked both sides of the legal street during his criminal career. He was one of America's most notorious smugglers and had also spent some time as a policeman in Seattle until he got involved with a counterfeiting ring there. He was brash and visible with his crimes, often to the point of being foolhardy. Terrible Terry was a complete opposite to the affable Bill Miner. But the men got along famously, and as a team they were a daunting criminal force.

Miner traveled south whenever his Princeton grubstake ran low to team with Terry in the smuggling business. They moved illegal Chinese immigrants and opium across the border with impunity for some time before Bill suggested to Terry that there was a faster way to score. They had trains in Canada too, didn't they? And unlike Colorado or Oregon, the territory around his Canadian bolthole didn't sport a gun-wielding sheriff in every town big enough to have a horse trough. Miner convinced Terry to use his extensive knowledge of train routes and schedules to plan a robbery while he looked for a suitable recruit for their gang.

Bill had a naïve mountain man in mind, someone who could lead an escape through the woods in areas that were unfamiliar. William "Shorty" Dunn fit the bill perfectly. Dunn was a stocky, dark-complexioned fellow who had moved to Canada from the United States years before to prospect in the Hedley area. He was an able woodsman who was working in a sawmill near Princeton when Bill began his recruiting mission. Shorty, a little slow but friendly, was an easy target for the cunning robber. Bill showered him with gifts and became a fixture near Shorty whenever he wasn't working. It was just a matter of time before Miner convinced Dunn to guide several hunting trips into the backcountry. Dunn also began to join Miner on the small cattle drives he undertook to supplement his income and to become familiar with the land surrounding his new safe house.

In September 1904, Bill and Shorty left Princeton on one of those trips, but instead of hunting game, they traveled south toward the U.S. border to rendezvous with Terry. Jake had done his homework and selected an ideal location, near Mission, British Columbia, to rob the Canadian Pacific Railway (CPR) Transcontinental Express No. 1.

Chapter 7
An Unscheduled Stop

t 9:30 p.m. on September 10, 1904, Miner, Terry, and Dunn waited in the dense fog at Mission Junction. Terry had tapped the telegraph wire, sending a message to the Mission Junction agent that purported to be from the railway's head office. His message claimed that the combination to the safe had been lost and ordered the agent to leave the safe in the express car unlocked. The CPR Transcontinental Express was already two-and-a-half hours late because of the near-zero visibility, so the railroad crew was distracted as they hastily worked at refilling the train's boiler at the water tower 197 yards west of the depot. It was an ideal circumstance for the robbers. They slipped onto the express unseen and hid in the blind baggage until the train started moving.

Terry, a skilled planner, had taken extra precautions. Each of the men wore a hood with slits cut for their eyes and floppy Stetsons pulled low to disguise themselves even more. They were armed with revolvers and a rifle and were roughly dressed. One last time, Terry reminded his partners not to use their real names during commission of the robbery as he led the way out of the baggage car and over the coal tender to the engine.

Engineer Nathaniel J. Scott jumped in surprise when a hand clamped on his shoulder and the business end of a revolver was pressed to his cheek. "Hands up!" Scott released his grip on the engine throttle in quick response to the soft southern drawl. Turning, he saw two masked bandits pointing revolvers and a third with a rifle trained on his fireman. "I want you to stop the train at Silverdale crossing," his captor said. "Do what you are told and not a hair of your head will be harmed." Scott knew Silverdale. It was a small siding roughly halfway between Mission and Whonnock. He nodded. "I am at your service."

Once the train slowed to a wheezing stop at Silverdale, Miner ordered the fireman to lead him to the express car. The unscheduled stop aroused the curiosity of brakeman Bill Abbott. As Miner and the fireman passed between a passenger car and the express car, Abbott poked his head out to see the cause.

"Get back inside unless you want your head blown off, and be quick!"

Abbott promptly did as he was told. He later recalled, "As I poked my head out of the car, I came face-to-face with a masked fellow holding a gun that looked as big as a sewer pipe." Without a moment's hesitation, he bolted through the train to the rear and leapt down to the tracks. In seconds Abbot had disappeared into the fog, heading back to Mission Junction for help. Abbott's leap from the train had created immediate panic among the passengers. One of them, in an attempt to discourage the bandits, fired three random shots into the fog while other passengers removed their jewelry and tried to find hiding places for their valuables.

Miner ducked behind the fireman at the sound of the gunshots and angrily ordered him to unhook the cars behind the express. This done, he retraced his steps back to the engine using Freeman as a shield. "Go to the Whonnock mile post and stop just in front of the church!" he shouted to Scott. "Do as you are told and no one will be hurt." Scott slowly eased the train forward, away from a now panicked group of passengers. Once he got to Whonnock, Miner left Dunn in the engine compartment to guard the fireman and forced Scott to guide him to the express car.

Miner tossed a rock at the door to rouse the express car messenger, Herb Mitchell. Mitchell opened his window to see Nate Scott.

"What do you want Nate?"

"Open up the door or the car will be blown up."

"Who's going to blow it up?"

"These fellows here."

Mitchell slammed the window tight and drew his .38 Smith & Wesson. Another express messenger inside, William Thorburn, stepped back from the door.

"Open up or we'll blow the door down with this dynamite," a calm voice said from the other side. Mitchell and Thorburn considered their alternatives. Reluctantly but obediently, the messengers slowly slid the door open. Mitchell found the barrel of Miner's revolver under his nose. "Put your hands up and come down."

When the men jumped to the ground, Terry pulled Mitchell's gun from its holster and passed it to Miner. "Do as you're told," Miner said, pressing his gun to Mitchell's nose, "and we won't hurt a hair of your head. It's not your money I want."

Miner climbed into the express looking for another guard, then searched for the safes. A large one had been left open, but a small one remained sealed. The big safe was empty. "Get back up here and open that safe!" Bill barked. The small safe held the consignment the robbers were expecting — $4000 in gold dust bound for Seattle, $2000 in gold dust for the Bank of British North America in Vancouver, and $1000 in cash.

Laughing with delight, Miner thanked Mitchell and shoved him back to the waiting attentions of Terry and Dunn, who were now also training their guns at the railroad men. Meticulously, Miner began searching the car and opening any registered mail he uncovered. To his repeated whistles of joy, he tossed $50,000 in U.S. bonds and an estimated $250,000 in Australian securities into a pile on the floor. When he was satisfied that he'd found everything of value, he dumped Mitchell's clothing out of his travel bag and stuffed the gold and securities inside.

"Now tell me where I'll find the treasure chest."

Mitchell shrugged his shoulders.

"We were expecting $62,000 in a treasure chest," Miner repeated. "It went by stage from the Consolidated Caribou Mine to Ashcroft, now where is it?"

"Oh *that* treasure chest," Mitchell answered. "Got delayed at the last so the bullion will be on a later train."

"Well, I guess this does it," Miner groaned as he hefted the travel bag and jumped from the car.

The bandits guided the railroad workers back to the engine, and as the final act in Terry's plan, pulled the fireman's coal shovel from the engine deck and threw it into the woods.

Miner told Scott he could return for his passengers.

"Happy journey," Scott replied.

"Be careful when you are backing up that you don't meet with some accident," Miner answered politely.

The engineer smiled at the advice. "You fellows have your nerve with you."

"Yes, and we have something else," Miner said lifting the bag. "Good night boys." With that, the bandits backed away into the fog. The entire robbery had taken only 30 minutes. The brakeman, Bill Abbott, had run to Mission Junction, but the agent there didn't believe his story so he failed to notify his superiors on the coast. After all, there had never been a robbery of a CPR train. With no other option, Scott stayed with his engine, and the coal-starved train limped into Vancouver a few hours later. Bill Miner had made history.

Chief Constable Colin Campbell of the British Columbia Provincial Police, and Superintendent H.E. Beasley, of the Canadian Pacific Railway Police, were swift to question the crew and passengers. They concluded that professionals had executed the robbery. As they had no experience with train robberies and because it was apparent the gang leader was an American, judging by his accent, the Canadian authorities called in Pinkerton's agency. Superintendent James E. Dye, head of Pinkerton's in Seattle, was still investigating the year-old hold-up near Portland of the Oregon Railway & Navigation Company's express train. He believed that the same men had committed both robberies. Dye dispatched detectives to the U.S. border, a little less than 10 miles from the robbery scene, to initiate a search. The CPR posted a reward of $5000 for the capture of the desperadoes, the Canadian government also put up $6000, and the government of British Columbia offered $500. This $11,500 reward for the capture of Canada's first train robbers was reported to be as much as 20 years worth of wages for the average Canadian laborer.

The British Columbia Provincial Police concentrated

their search on the area around Abbotsford. A boat had been found at Whonnock and scrutiny of the riverbank indicated that three men had moved from it toward Lynden, Washington, a small farming community settled by Dutch immigrants. However, the footprints disappeared in the area of Sumas. Several men who looked suspicious were arrested and then released. Three men had been tracked to a homesteader's cabin, but they could prove they were in Seattle the night of the robbery. Another man who'd been in the district for weeks without apparent purpose was arrested as well, but he turned out to be a detective working on another case. It's no wonder then that by late September when an independent tracker claimed to have found the trail of three men heading toward Princeton, the lawmen ignored the report and continued searching the border area instead. They were obviously tired and frustrated.

Dye felt certain the failed Oregon Railway & Navigation Company robbery was Bill Miner's handiwork. He was the only criminal in Pinkerton's files who was consistently polite to his victims, and most telling, the robber had used the expression "Hands up!" which was Miner's trademark. "I was positive," said Dye later, "that Bill Miner was the mastermind behind the Portland train robbery and the hold-up at Mission Junction in British Columbia." Dye hadn't considered that Miner might have fled to Canada because it didn't fit his profile. But flush with cash from the Mission Junction robbery, that is precisely what Bill, Jake, and Shorty did.

Miner resumed his role as a southern gentleman of leisure in Princeton, more confident than ever in the safety of his Canadian hideaway.

Princeton Station Agent W.R. Nelews would later remember just how comfortable Miner had made his life in Princeton.

> *[He] used to spend about three hours every day grooming and training his beautiful white horse named Pat. I believe no one could have a greater love for his mate than each had for the other. Pat had an intelligence of a very high order. Miner had a specially constructed watch, whose dial letters were raised, and had trained his horse to tell the time by stamping his feet. Bill was a great favourite with children. Saturday afternoons, weather permitting, Bill and Pat, followed by a bunch of girls and boys, would go to the outskirts of Princeton and the children would be given tickets for a free ride on Pat. Pat took as much pleasure from these rides as the children did.*

Whenever Bill disappeared on a business trip, usually taking Shorty along for company, no one took notice of it in Princeton. Nor did they connect him to crimes that always seemed to coincide elsewhere when he was away. In October 1905, for example, the Great Northern Railway was held up at the Raymond brickyard near Ballard and Ravenna Park (later a suburb of Seattle). The three masked men who committed that robbery netted a $36,000 pay-off for their efforts.

Bill Miner and Shorty Dunn had left Princeton at the end of September and likely met up with Jake Terry in Bellingham. The trio made their way to Seattle where they met James "Lem" Short, an acquaintance of Terry's. On the night of October 2, the bandits severed the telephone wires at Kirkland. Terry and Dunn positioned themselves near the train tracks at Ballard while Miner took the wagon to Interbay and boarded the Great Northern train. Just as he'd done before, Miner climbed over the coal tender and surprised the engineer and fireman. He politely instructed them to continue their trip until they spotted a signal fire and to stop the train there.

In a *Seattle Post–Intelligencer* newspaper report after the robbery, the fireman described the first bandit as a tall man with a stoop. When the train stopped, he said another shorter man climbed aboard and gave them orders. The men had referred to each other as Tom and Bill. "Damn the luck!" Bill groused after finding nothing of value lying about in the express car. The fireman, a man named Julette, strained to hear what the two bandits were saying to each other in the car as they rifled through the bags. He made out "... this is as bad as ..." but no more. (Miner may have been referring to his embarrassing time with LeRoy.) Then the bandits tackled the tough job of blowing the express car safe. Miner leaned dynamite on the safe door, lit the fuse — and with Terry beside him — jumped from the car. When the smoke cleared, they looked in to find the safe undamaged.

Miner thrust a stick of dynamite into Julette's hands. "You get up there and blow that safe open!"

The fireman did as he was told but like the first attempt, the blast only scorched the door. "Give me the damn dynamite!" Terry shouted at Miner. He set the third charge himself and this time the safe shattered. "Get in there and pick up the loot!" Terry commanded the fireman. As Julette did the bandit's bidding, Miner moved to both sides of the train firing warning shots down the track to keep curious passengers in their seats. When Julette handed over the booty, the two bandits backed away and vanished into the darkness.

The head of Pinkerton's Seattle bureau, P.K. Ahearn, was convinced, by the manner of the robbery, that the crime was a patented Miner job. This added to Pinkerton's contention that Bill Miner was now operating in Oregon and Washington. Instead of actively investigating the robbery, the agency decided to wait out the robbers, hoping that sooner or later they would find a stool pigeon.

Chapter 8
"No Prison Walls Can Hold Me"

n apparent lack of interest on the part of Pinkerton's National Detective Agency in searching for the robbers of the Great Northern Railway bolstered Miner's belief that he was safe in Canada. Miner, however, had a problem. The bonds and securities taken in the Mission Junction robbery were negotiable, but any attempt to cash them would expose his whereabouts. He convinced Dunn and Terry that the bonds held no value unless they could somehow be liquidated in a third-party fashion. His partners agreed that he should dispose of the paper securities any way he liked.

According to all the American newspaper reports, Bill Miner had been listed as a prime suspect in the robbery. As far as Miner was concerned, that only meant he had to be sure to maintain his cover as kindly Bill Edwards in Princeton. Bill had delayed destroying the bonds and, as there had been no suspicions broadcast about Jake Terry's involvement in the robbery, Bill came up with what he considered a cunning plan. If Terry could strike a deal to act as an intermediary for the return of the securities, he may be able to demand a commission, which the three men could then split. Terry agreed to give it a try.

Terry made a brazen announcement to the authorities. He openly admitted he was Bill Miner's close friend and said that he knew his old San Quentin cellmate had committed the robbery. Terry offered to act as a go-between with Miner to arrange the return of the bonds — for a fee. Neither the CPR nor the government took the bait.

Bill decided to lay low when the plan fizzled. Terry had recently been arrested for assault in Port Townsend and Miner probably worried about his partner's loyalty. Rather than sit about waiting for the law to pounce (should Terry be coerced into talking), Bill took Shorty farther into the British Columbia interior. The men worked for a time on the Douglas Lake cattle ranch and ran a few head of their own around Aspen Grove, 12 miles from Merritt. In the latter part of 1905 or early 1906, they returned to the Budd ranch, confident in Terry's silence.

When Louis Colquhoun, a 29-year-old former school teacher from Clifford, Ontario, showed up in Princeton, he found a ready welcome among Bill's tiny entourage at the

Budd ranch. Colquhoun had contracted tuberculosis in eastern Canada and several years before had traveled west to find a more pleasant climate. His journey took him to Vancouver, San Francisco, and eventually the State of Washington where a petty theft, landed him in the Walla Walla Penitentiary for a two-year stint. After that he wandered north to Bill Miner's quiet retreat in Princeton.

Miner, still calling himself George Edwards, had gained a reputation in the Similkameen country of being rather eccentric. He was known to be a likeable fellow who never seemed short of cash or the penchant for talking about his gold mines in Argentina. He smoked foul-smelling "black strap" tobacco in his pipe and often functioned in a euphoric daze. His acquaintances put the odd behavior down to the opium pills that he'd taken to chewing. Edwards called them his "poppy root." Although opium was a legal substance in Canada at the time, most people shunned it because of its addictive affect. It was also very costly, but that didn't seem to stop Edwards from having a constant supply.

In early 1906, Bill strayed from Princeton, leaving his confederates on the Budd Ranch. He made his way back to Aspen Grove where, for two months, he bunked with a farmer named Alonzo Roberts. He spent his time leisurely riding the hills and hunting. By March, Bill was bored and ready for some action. So when Shorty Dunn and Louis Colquhoun arrived in Aspen Grove to invite the older man on a prospecting trip, Bill was eager to join. Or so it appeared to his host Alonzo Roberts.

Bill told Roberts that Dunn and Colquhoun wanted to try their luck prospecting in the creeks between Merritt and Princeton. The announcement was completely believable. Rumours had been flying about in the Similkameen for months that prospectors had found shows of the yellow metal in creeks around the Grand Prairie area (now known as Westwold), 81 miles north of Princeton. On March 28, Bill added credence to the announcement by visiting the McFadden ranch in Princeton and borrowing a dark bay and a pinto to be used as pack animals.

Perhaps Dunn and Colquhoun had genuinely wanted to prospect because it took the trio until April 29 to reach Ducks (now known as Monte Creek), a way station on the CPR about 15 miles east of Kamloops. Had they left with a robbery in mind, it was a distance they could have covered much more quickly. Or, perhaps it was only part of an elaborate plan Miner had concocted to cloak their activities with a believable alibi after a robbery. Regardless, Bill and his partners remained encamped at Ducks until May 8 and made a point of socializing with the locals. They even bought supplies for their "prospecting" at William Cubbs' small general store, while discussing the possible danger of wildfire. Trees were already ablaze in the mountains north of Ducks, filling the valleys south of it with a thick smoky haze.

Because of the smoke, May 8 was a rather dark day

and a foggy veil lay over the countryside. Engineer J. Callin had been carefully coaxing the CPR Imperial Limited No. 97 through the smoke and had stopped his train as he routinely did at Ducks. When he resumed his journey, he'd been concentrating on the route so carefully he didn't notice the man who climbed into the engine cab until he felt the barrel of a revolver in the small of his back. "Hands up!" Callin turned to see who had given the order. The bandit was middle-aged and was wearing a buggy looking set of goggles and a bandana. Miner prodded him with the revolver again. "I want you to stop the train at Mile Post 116. Don't do anything foolish, and you won't be hurt."

At the given spot, Miner forced Callin and his fireman, Radcliffe, to uncouple the engine and the first car from the train. Then he had them carry on another couple of miles. Callin did as he was directed and watched as two more bandits scampered from the grass toward him. One was a short, muscular man with a red handkerchief over his face. The other hadn't taken the same precaution. The neck of his sweater was tugged up to his nose and the cloth cap on his head did a poor job of hiding the rest of his face. But Callin didn't spend much time on that. The third man carried a package wrapped in newspaper and the engineer could see the butts of several dynamite sticks protruding from it.

"Let's take a walk to the express car."

Callin and Radcliffe led the way to the first car behind the coal tender and rapped on the door. The unarmed express messenger inside, who was unlucky enough to be in the same situation during the Mission Junction robbery, got out of his chair and leaned at the door to listen.

"We're being robbed," Bill Thorburn whispered to his mail clerk partner, A.L. McQuarrie, as he strained to hear what was being said outside on the track. Thorburn recognized one of the voices and that awareness sent a flush of shivers rising from his neck. When the tap came on his door again with another gruff command to open it, Thorburn was absolutely certain. In the hold-up a year earlier he had managed to avoid being fired when the CPR fired his co-worker Herb Mitchell. It hadn't been Mitchell's fault, but their angry CPR employers decided to make an example of him for co-operating too readily with robbers. There was no way Thorburn wanted the same treatment. He simply refused to open the door.

"Open it, I say, or we'll blow it!" Miner ordered.

"Open it," McQuarrie pleaded.

Thorburn, now resigned to what was about to happen, slowly slipped the latch and slid the door open. He pulled his own cap forward over his face before he leaped to the ground so the robber waiting beside the track wouldn't have a chance to see who he was. After searching the mail clerks for weapons, Miner motioned with his revolver for McQuarrie to climb back aboard.

"You're somewhat ahead of your time. We didn't expect you for another hour. It's lucky we were waiting."

"We're on summer schedule," McQuarrie answered. "The train runs two sections and this is the first one."

In the yellow glow of coal oil lamps, Miner started rifling through the car looking for registered mail. "Where is the shipment for San Francisco, the registered mail for Frisco?" Miner had learned about a rich shipment of money and bonds coming through Kamloops, which was destined for San Francisco. San Francisco had just suffered a devastating earthquake and Canadians had rallied to provide financial and material support. The relief cash was supposed to be on the train. McQuarrie told him there wasn't any to be found in the baggage car.

"Baggage car?" Miner cursed in frustration. He stamped a foot and shook his head violently enough to dislodge his bandana. McQuarrie got a good look at Miner's face with its droopy gray moustache before the old bandit leaned out of the car to speak to his confederates. He told them the express car had been switched with the baggage car and that the express car was still coupled to the passenger cars down the track.

The engine was backed up to a steady stream of cursing from Miner, but he composed himself as the steam engine approached the express and passenger cars. "Well, let's see what's here," he said, climbing aboard with a heavy groan. He ripped open the postal sacks with angry determination looking for registered mail, never thinking to examine anything else. He found 11 letters, but his smile evaporated when they contained a paltry $15.50. Spotting a box of catarrh pills, Bill scooped them up and with a curt nod ordered his two partners away.

Miner had the engineers move the train to a spot between Mile Post 119 and 120 before he and his partners jumped to the gravel ballast beside the track and ran for the bush. "Good night, boys," he said to the railroad crew, obviously disappointed. "Take care of yourself."

With those departing words, he too ran into the darkness.

When the bandits were gone, Callin looked at Thorburn. The two mail clerks had been left standing beside the express car. "What are you smilin' about?" Thorburn burst out laughing. "See those packages on the shelf? That's $40,000 in bank notes and he didn't even look at them!"

The take from the robbery wouldn't even have paid for a weekend of carousing in Kamloops, but the British Columbia Provincial Police reacted as though Miner had found that large amount of cash instead of the liver pills.

The next day, William L. Fernie, a provincial police officer recognized as a top tracker, along with two Native scouts, Ignace and Michael, mounted up and were on Miner's trail like bloodhounds. Fernie found the gang's dynamite at the robbery site, still wrapped in a *Kamloops Inland Sentinel* newspaper with a mailing label to an Aspen Grove subscriber. He also found footprints. There were two sets of hobnailed boots and another set that looked almost as if they'd been made for a woman. Within a few hours they tracked the prints to the camp the men had made before their robbery.

"Men are out in every direction and all the roads and trails north and south, through the Nicola and Okanagan districts, are watched," the *Kamloops Inland Sentinel* reported on its front page, only days after the robbery. "A number of Pinkerton detectives came in from Seattle yesterday and have joined in the chase. F.S. Hussey, superintendent of provincial police, arrived here last night to take charge of affairs and railway detectives and officials are also in the city, directing the search and placing all their resources at the command of the police."

Because of the fire north of Ducks, Fernie focused on a likely escape route south toward Douglas Lake. The scouts soon uncovered the tracks of two packhorses that led them to another campsite in a meadow. The campsite afforded a clear view of the CPR tracks. Fernie carefully examined the hoof prints. It seemed the packhorses had either been released or escaped because, without a doubt, the three men he was pursuing had headed out of the camp on foot.

While at Campbell's Meadows, Fernie was joined by another constable named Pierce who reported that on May 9 a man, J. Greaves of Douglas Lake Ranch, had spotted two horses. One was hobbled in the American fashion and the other, a pinto, was hobbled Native style. At least one of the men was a savvy backwoodsman, Fernie reasoned.

The officers followed the three sets of tracks south over

rocky ground, which made the pursuit tedious and time consuming. By their direction, Fernie decided the men were making for the old Hudson's Bay Trail that would eventually lead across the mountain divide and into the Nicola Valley. Convinced the three were headed toward the United States, Fernie reported his progress. On May 11, Superintendent F.S. Hussy of the British Columbia Provincial Police decided to call on the North West Mounted Police (NWMP) in Calgary for help.

A small party of four Mounties, under the command of Sergeant J.J. Wilson, was immediately dispatched from Alberta by train. Wilson stopped in Morley and in Banff to add two more officers, making a squad of seven pursuers. They arrived at Kamloops in mid-afternoon the next day, and were outfitted with untrained horses and a scout named Slim Jim Benyon. Ostensibly, their job was to ride south in the driving rain to catch the robbers before they crossed the border. So, with their fresh mounts, they galloped into unknown territory.

Despite the weather, Fernie and his scouts doggedly continued to follow the tracks they'd found. Time was going to be their enemy. Rainfall made the tracks almost impossible to see. Fernie was afraid that once the bandits left the treed mountainous area and reached the plains approaching the Nicola Valley, the tracks would become impossible to recognize. Fernie sent Pierce toward Grand Prairie just in case he'd guessed wrong about the escape route. On May

14, his diligence paid off. He spotted his three quarries near Douglas Lake.

"I was moving rather slowly, while keeping a sharp look-out for the bandits, when suddenly I came upon them," Fernie reported. "They had not seen me, so to be sure of their identity I went back upon their trail until I assured myself that the tracks were the same as I had been following from the scene of the hold-up. There they were, the two with hob-nailed boots and the slim womanish smooth shoes of the third."

Fernie perhaps was tracing the footprints a little too obviously because his actions appeared suspicious to his suspects. When he suddenly realized they had spotted him, he decided to approach their camp nonchalantly. Because Fernie was wearing civilian clothes, Miner would not allow Dunn to take aim at their unwelcome guest. The policeman must have looked as tired and bedraggled as his quarries did in the heavy rain.

"Which is the way to Quilchena?" Bill asked Fernie as the officer drew near, trying to give the impression he was as unlucky as Fernie seemed to be.

Fernie pointed out the direction to him and said, "Am I on the right road for Chapperon?"

"It's back the other way," Bill replied.

The officer cussed as if he'd just wasted his time riding the wrong way and asked the trio from where they'd come.

"Oh, we're prospectors," Bill said with a pleasant conversational tone. "We've been to Grand Prairie."

Fernie asked if they'd had any luck. He noted that a dark mood was suddenly apparent on the older man's face as he replied that they had not.

Thanking them for their help, Fernie turned his horse and fought the urge to gallop away. He fully expected a bullet in his back. When he was out of sight, however, he put the spurs to his horse. At the first ranch he encountered, he borrowed a fresh mount and raced to Chapperon Lake where he knew the NWMP officer, Sergeant Wilson, would be waiting.

Wilson deployed three of his men to high ground hoping they might be able to spot the robbers. With the remaining four men he made a full-speed seven-mile dash from Chapperon Lake to the suspects' camp. It took them just 20 minutes. Fernie, who had been tracking for days without sleep, was not entirely certain about where he'd talked to the robbers, so the NWMP officers scattered into the bush hunting for tracks. When one of the officers spotted campfire smoke, he waved his hat to draw in the others. Then Wilson attempted a capture. He had his men encircle the group on foot and then he approached the camp alone. Wilson carried a hat that had been found at the robbery site and he dropped it as he slowly walked toward the men.

"Hello the camp," he said cautiously when he had them in sight.

Miner waved in greeting.

"Where are you boys in from?'

"Across the river," Miner replied, "from over there." He

pointed in the direction of Campbell's Meadow where Fernie had first found boot tracks.

"That right?" Sergeant Wilson asked. "I was there not long back but didn't see you. How long ago was it?"

"Two days."

Wilson then identified himself as an NWMP sergeant. "There was a train robbery at Ducks and I'm in pursuit," he said. "What are you boys doing here?"

"Prospecting a little," Shorty Dunn replied.

"Who are you?"

"I'm George Edwards," Bill answered. "This is Billy Dunn and the tall one is Louis Colquhoun."

"What are you doing here?"

"Prospecting," echoed an unperturbed Miner. "We started over at Aspen Grove and worked our way toward Grand Prairie and we haven't had any luck, so we're on our way back to Princeton."

Wilson debated with himself. He knew that Fernie, who'd been tracking the robbers, was exhausted. In following the train robbers he had covered nearly 187 miles in three days and nights. Perhaps he had identified this group incorrectly. The trio, after all, didn't act like wanted men. Sergeant Wilson thanked them and calmly turned to leave. As he walked away from the camp he pretended to spot the hat he'd dropped, as if for the first time.

"To which of you does this belong?"

Bill stood up and moved to retrieve the hat. Wilson

sidled backward to a spot where he had all three men in easy view. "You answer the description given of the train robbers," he said slowly, "and we arrest you for that crime."

Miner answered the charge with a hearty laugh. "We do not look much like train robbers," he protested merrily.

Shorty Dunn, however, was less able to hide his fear. Scanning the brush, he spotted another lawman and rolled away from the campfire, drawing his revolver. "Look out boys, it's all up!" he shouted, firing into the brush.

Wilson drew his revolver on Miner and another officer emerged from the trees pointing his gun at Colquhoun. As Dunn crashed through the underbrush in panic, the three other officers gave chase, firing as they ran. Dunn shot back. After 20 bullets whizzed through the trees, he suddenly screamed, "I'm shot!" and plunged into a ditch. The officers pounced, relieved Dunn of his guns, and dragged him back to the camp with a bullet wound dripping from the calf of one leg.

"That was a foolish trick," Sergeant Wilson admonished. "You may have been shot in the head just as easy."

"I wish to God you had put it through my head, but you couldn't blame me could you?" Wilson confiscated the men's weapons and had them turn out their pockets. Miner had $26. Dunn and Colquhoun only small change, but Wilson also found a bottle of catarrh pills and a set of goggles among Miner's things. Convinced by that evidence, he had the trio tied up. A stoneboat (a low sledge with runners made of logs) that had been abandoned nearby was employed as a stretcher for Dunn. Sergeant Wilson then marched his captives through the rain to the Douglas Lake ranch.

When they reached the ranch, Greaves, the man who'd spotted the hobbled horses days earlier, told the police they'd made a mistake. They were holding Mr. Bill Edwards of Princeton, a well-known rancher, he told them. Mr. Edwards is certainly not at all the type to rob trains, Greaves said with confidence. Sergeant Wilson insisted the truth of that fact would soon be a matter for a judge to decide. He commandeered a buckboard (a horse-drawn vehicle with the body formed by a plank fixed to the axles) and conveyed his charges to Quilchena. Shorty Dunn's wound, though nasty, was not life threatening. Dr. Tuhill from Nicola treated the gunshot wound that evening, and the next morning Sergeant Wilson and his group began their long buckboard ride to Kamloops.

Late on the afternoon of May 15, 1906, during a torrential downpour, the men arrived in Kamloops. More interest couldn't have been raised if the wagon had carried an exotic circus animal. News of Wilson's success had preceded him from Quilchena and a crowd of a thousand lined the muddy street as the wagon splashed its way to the jail. Miner, who had wrapped himself in a blanket with his head covered, refused to satisfy their curiosity.

"On Wednesday afternoon at half-past-four a thousand people stood in the rain to watch a bedraggled cavalcade jogging down the hills back of the town," the *Kamloops Standard* later reported. The newspaper described Miner as "a striking looking fellow with grizzled hair and moustache, erect and active and does not appear to bear within ten years of the weight of age which the prison records now credit him with."

The *Similkameen Star* on May 19 described Bill differently. "Edwards had none of the swagger, 'blow' or bluff of the would-be desperado or tough; in conversation he was pleasant and of considerable polish of manner. He never made any gun play although he always carried a brace of shooters, a common thing with men on the frontier."

Miner may have thought he could confuse matters by insisting he was George Edwards, but that didn't last long. The day after the men arrived in Kamloops, Constable J.T. Browning recalled the Mission Junction robber-wanted poster. He examined George Edwards for tattoos. On finding them he, of course, contacted Pinkerton's men. By the following day a prison photograph was the final stroke against Miner's phoney identity. From it, the CPR mail clerk, A.L. McQuarrie, positively identified Miner as one of the Mile 16 train robbers. The .38 Smith & Wesson taken from Miner by Wilson was also identified as the gun stolen from mail clerk Mitchell during the 1904 robbery at Mission, British Columbia.

The San Quentin warden drove the final nail. He had also made it to Kamloops to assist in the identification and confirmed that the man calling himself Edwards was none other than Bill Miner. Warden Kelly even extended a hand to Miner when he made the identification.

"I'll shake hands with you all right, but I don't know you," Miner said caustically.

The next morning the trio was brought before the Kamloops mayor for a preliminary hearing on evidence. Attorney General Fulton conducted the prosecution of the case while Kamloops lawyer Alex D. McIntyre was employed as the defense counsel. The mayor found the evidence overwhelming and promptly bound the men over for trial. Sergeant Wilson and four of his NWMP constables, as well as William Fernie, were paid the $11,500 reward that had been posted for the capture of the fugitives — for the theft of $15.50 and some liver pills.

Eleven days later, Miner, Dunn, and Colquhoun faced a trial. The presiding justice, P.A.E. Irving, was firmly convinced of their guilt. But the jury was less certain. After four hours of deliberation the jury stood at seven for conviction and five for acquittal. They asked for excerpts of the testimony and then retired for another seven hours. The jury foreman, 65-year-old J. Morrill, held out for an acquittal. He had been heard to say he didn't believe a poor man should ever be sent to prison. Rather than release the culprits, however, another jury was empanelled for a second trial on June 1. That case was presented in just two hours.

Throughout the second trial Shorty Dunn became hysterical, often shouting uncontrollably, to the point where a prison physician was called to calm him. The new jury deliberated for only 30 minutes before returning a guilty verdict.

The *Similkameen Star* reported Miner's attitude for its subscribers on June 2. "As to his socialistic ideas announced by a coast paper, he never openly declared himself to those who met him frequently here, but his actions seem to indicate that he believed in a division of wealth in which 'Old Bill' would get rather more than half. He always expressed great antipathy for capital, but here again his actions pointed to an unlawful desire to become a capitalist quickly."

When Judge Irving asked the prisoners if they had anything to say before sentence was passed, they all replied no. Judge Irving then said, "The case against you was very clear. I agree with the verdict and the sentence of this court is that you, George Edwards, be confined in the penitentiary for life, you William Dunn for life, and you Louis Colquhoun, for twenty-five years." Bill Miner accepted a life sentence, for the theft of $15.50 and a box of liver pills, with a cold stare. At the declaration, Dunn reportedly broke into tears. Miner then faced the judge.

"No prison walls can hold me," he said with malicious warning.

The next day, heavily shackled, the trio was marched to the railway station through a crowd of rubberneckers. Many were sympathetic to the elder bandit, calling to him with best wishes. Some thrust cigars in his hands like they were old friends. In their opinion, the robbers hadn't committed a crime worthy of a life sentence by robbing the CPR. After all, they joked, the CPR "robs us every day."

The Billy Miner myth seemed to gain popular appeal as his train rolled west. Bill Miner never robbed the poor man, people observed. He only preyed on corporations. He was a kindly "gentleman bandit," they told each other. He gave to the poor. For that he deserved leniency. When Bill's guards were notified that a large, noisy crowd was waiting to receive the criminal like a hero at the New Westminster depot, a decision was made to put the prisoners off at Sapperton. But word of that ploy leaked. At Sapperton an even larger crowd gathered, giving the arrival a clamorous circus-like atmosphere. Bill didn't welcome the applause. In Kamloops he was called Mr. Edwards, he said, "but down here even the dogs seem to take me for Bill Miner."

Chapter 9
A Very Strange Jailbreak

iner's cell in the New Westminster prison gave him a clear view of the CPR tracks that ran past the penitentiary. It was an ironic add-on to the punishment for the old bandit. The penitentiary, poorly built by the government, had opened on September 28, 1878. However, in comparison to the inhumane conditions of his San Quentin home five years earlier, the British Columbia Penitentiary had all the confining terror of a ranch house.

Only a wooden wall and a low wooden fence separated the men from society and both were often collapsing. There were no hardened guards with truncheons, no tortuous "hole" for troublemakers. In fact, the morale of the prison attendants was lower than that of the convicts because of incompetent administrators who ran the prison without the benefit of clear policies on conduct.

If there ever was a prison that was ripe for a Bill Miner escape, it was the New West Pen. With that low level of security in mind, however, and because of his courtroom declaration, Bill was placed in close confinement for the first part of his incarceration there.

For a time he was allowed no visitors except for the daughter of the deputy warden. Catherine Bourke was drawn to the iconic outlaw in a zealous personal quest to reform him through the Word of God. Bill welcomed her attentions and easily manipulated her influence on her father to his benefit. With charm and apparent sincerity, he convinced Catherine he was a harmless aged outlaw who finally had seen the light through her ministrations and Bible readings. She reacted with sympathy, convincing her father and the warden to loosen Bill's chains.

Miner was moved into the general population and put to work in the prison shoe factory because of the training he'd received in San Quentin. Bill went to work making a special pair of boots for his bad feet. Strangely, he was granted additional privileges that the other convicts were not allowed. For instance, Bill was given permission to meet with his defense lawyer, Alex McIntyre, whenever he wished. Other prisoners were allowed no such privilege. He was allowed to grow his hair while his prison mates went about with their head's shaved. And he was free to write more than one letter a month.

On February 8, 1907, Miner met with his lawyer Alex McIntyre, the warden, J.C. Whyte, a detective from the CPR police, and his old partner Jake Terry. The detective's objective was to talk about a pardon in exchange for the missing securities from the Mission Junction robbery. Terry had no idea where Bill had hidden the documents, but having been jailed for assault in the U.S., he tried to use his intervention in the matter to get a reprieve. A string of meetings in the following months culminated with one in July. Inspector Dawson of the Inspectors of Penitentiaries Office in Ottawa attended this meeting, but it seemed Miner was not willing to do an exchange for money. Instead, he wanted to be released and demanded a written guarantee before he gave up the ransomed securities.

Documenting proof of such a deal would be too politically dangerous for the CPR or the government should it ever be discovered, so Dawson refused. Whether it was Miner or the CPR who came up with an alternative solution to the impasse may never be known. But it appears a solution was agreed upon nevertheless, by what soon happened.

On the afternoon of August 9, 1907, Miner was given the job of delivering bricks from the prison brickyard to the drying kiln. He had to move the blocks by wheelbarrow, taking alternating turns in the heavy duty with other men. There were 29 men in that part of the prison on that Friday. James Doyle, an 18-year veteran as a prison guard, supervised 21 of the men in making the bricks. Bill and seven others were under the watchful eyes of another guard at the drying kiln. Overlooking the brick kiln, in a watchtower more than 164 feet high, a third guard viewed the yard. From the lookout tower, a walkway ran at a right angle on top of the wall for about 44 yards. The guard was supposed to patrol it every two minutes.

None of the guards seemed to be expecting trouble that day. After each trip, once he'd dropped his load of bricks at the kiln, Miner would stop at the prison's wooden fence to rest. His sympathetic guards thought nothing of the pause made by the aged convict. His younger shift mates knew better. It wasn't long before three of them realized what Miner was doing. On each of his rest stops, Bill was digging a hole under the fence. Before long, the other prisoners were also taking a rest and joining in on his landscaping. Apparently, the guard supervising the men in the yard failed to notice their rest breaks. The guard who patrolled the walkway didn't notice either. After several hours of furtive digging by the convicts, the tower–walkway guard decided to take an unauthorized cigarette break and the prisoners acted. Led by Bill, they belly-crawled through the shallow pit they'd excavated under the inner fence and ran into a compound between it and the outer 13-foot wall. One of the men quickly broke into a work shed with a pickax that happened to be lying nearby. In another odd coincidence, the same man found a ladder. Within a few seconds, the prisoners scampered up the ladder and over the wall to freedom.

The guard for the brick makers was the first to notice

that the wheelbarrow squad was missing. He fired his revolver at 4:00 p.m. to warn of the jailbreak, but it wasn't until 4:30 p.m. that a pursuit was organized. For some reason, it took a half-hour to identify who was missing and to get the remaining prisoners returned to their cells.

On the other side of the wall, the escapees scampered for cover, but Miner refused to run with them. They planned on finding safe haven in Vancouver, but Bill purposefully fled in a different direction as the prison bell finally sounded the alarm.

Deputy Warden D. D. Bourke, who was in charge of the penitentiary at the time, did not appear to be upset by the escape. As he dispatched pursuers, he confidently declared his guards would have all the convicts back in custody within 24 hours. Just a week before, Miner had asked Bourke for his outside work assignment, complaining that standing all day in the leather shop was aggravating his seriously debilitating foot condition. As proof, Miner had shown his bare feet to his jailer, who could see they were obviously in terrible shape. Thus, Bourke didn't feel that Miner would be able to travel far or fast on crippled feet. He expected Bill to be the first prisoner recovered.

Every police center in British Columbia and Washington State was alerted within hours. Pinkerton's detectives in Seattle were more suspicious of the wily old convict than Bourke. They immediately circulated their description of Bill Miner, the outlaw.

"William A. Miner, alias William Morgan, alias William Anderson; Canadian, occupation shoemaker, weight 138 pounds. Miner's distinguishing marks are on his forearm and were made by a tattooing needle and Indian Ink when he was a youngster; carries a tattoo at the base of thumb of left hand; also a heart pierced with a dagger; a ballet girl is tattooed on his right forearm and also a star; both wrist bones are large; has a mole in center of chest; mole under left breast and another on his right shoulder; another star tattooed on outside of calf on left leg; a discoloration on left buttock; a scar on his left shin; a scar on his right knee. A mole on his left shoulder blade. Two small scars on his neck. His face is potted and he wears both upper and lower false teeth."

Bourke realized soon enough he was only partly right about the recapture of the prisoners. By nightfall, Miner's three comrades were arrested in their old Vancouver haunts, but a search into the night had still not yielded a clue about Miner. Bourke began to worry that should Miner somehow make good his escape and reach his friends in Princeton, he'd find ready hiding places and might never be retrieved. To be safe, he ordered a close watch put on Jack Budd's ranch, but to Bourke's chagrin, Miner never appeared.

At five o'clock on the morning after the jailbreak, prison officials employed a bloodhound that readily picked up Miner's scent heading north. This could mean that Miner was making for Burrard Inlet and would very likely steal a boat or hop a train for the B.C. interior. Because of this possibility, a guard was placed on every road leading out of New Westminster. It seemed impossible for a man in prison garb to vanish with a security net so quickly placed around the city, but that is exactly what happened with Bill. It was as if a waiting accomplice had picked him up because the hound that had been steadily following him quite suddenly lost his scent while crossing a field, and didn't regain it.

Newspaper reporters began asking questions about the miraculous vanishing act. They intimated that prison officials had deliberately allowed the old outlaw to escape — but didn't boldly state their contention until February — six months later.

"The conclusion come to at the time," the *Daily Columbian* reported, "was that the convicts escaped through a hole which had been dug under the wall, and which was subsequently detected, but this theory has long since been discarded. Nearly every detective and police officer who inspected the hole said it was impossible for a man to get through it."

The reporters questioned how easily the tunnel under the fence had been dug — and without being noticed. It was also suspected that Bill had tucked thousands of dollars away as a hedge against an escape and that he was hidden in a New Westminster home until the search was called off. Another newspaper reporter echoed that claim with quotes from local residents. "Not only would nine-tenths of the people of the Nicola and Similkameen not betray Miner were he there, but they are proud of the fact that here is wide-open welcome for him ..."

The escape became regular grist for the newspapers and they seized the opportunity to ridicule and accuse authorities over the matter. The claim of collusion began to raise a public furore. More questions were asked about Miner's escape tunnel. It was curious how three other convicts, all in good health, could have been so easily rounded up only hours after their escape while Miner, hobbled with bad feet, had been able to outmanoeuvre search parties that included blood hounds.

Even though an official investigation into the escape concluded there had been no co-operation or collusion by prison officials, the suspicions didn't go away. Criticism of the prison administration continued to build. Finally, it culminated in accusations that prison security was lax and discipline below par at the New Westminster Penitentiary during Deputy Warden Bourke's tenure. Fault for the escape was laid in the deputy warden's lap. Bourke erupted in indignation.

On January 29, 1909, Bourke denied those allegations and threatened his superiors that unless his name was cleared officially, he would "open up a new field for moral reformers by telling the world the truth about the escape of Bill Miner."

Bourke's statement prompted J.D. Taylor, member of parliament for New Westminster and managing director of the *Daily Columbian,* to raise the matter in the House of Commons. On February 11, Taylor referred to rumours that, not only had the gates been left open, but also a guard had actually passed Miner money. He called for another public inquiry. Taylor launched a blistering attack of questions on the solicitor general in Parliament. The government politician replied he knew very little about the Miner case. But Taylor continued the pressure. The case was too important to be whitewashed, he said, accusing the solicitor general of hiding facts about the case from Parliament. Taylor elaborated in a newspaper editorial, "Mr. Aylesworth [the minister of justice] disposed of ... the story of the search for securities as an incentive to secure Miner's release ... "

It's possible that, in his response to threats to expose those at fault in the matter, Deputy Warden Bourke was "allowed to retire." The forced departure was, evidently, the final straw for Bourke. Even a retirement allowance of $279.23 a year was not enough to remedy his injured pride. He wrote a letter to the *Daily Columbian* on March 3, confirming suspicions that a deal may have been struck with Miner.

"On one occasion the previous summer, 1906, Bill Miner was sent for to go to the Warden's office ... He said that he met in the warden's office the warden, the lawyer McIntyre who defended him, CPR Detective Bullock, and an old pal of [Miner's] named Terry ... that after a brief conversation the warden went out of the office, [and] that on the wardens going out ... Detective Bullock made an offer of a pardon [for]

Miner if he revealed where the hidden bonds were and [said] that the CPR would get him the pardon. Miner agreed to this, but wanted a guarantee that the pardon would be forthcoming. The detective could give him no guarantee other than his verbal promise. This Miner would not accept and the interview ended."

The public was enraged that a corporation, even if it was the revered CPR, might have been able to influence justice in that way. The argument pushed the matter up the political food chain. Opposition leader, R.L. Borden finally stood in Parliament and said that the deputy warden should be summoned before a committee of Parliament and compelled to provide answers on the whole affair. Of course, the government objected. The minister of justice called all the rumours unfounded and dismissed them. But the solicitor general slipped up in questioning and admitted that a guard had resigned after it was discovered he'd been passing on notes written by Miner. He also admitted that Miner had meetings with detectives about the Australian securities, thus confirming Bourke's allegations.

How is that possible, asked other parliamentarians, when the regulations only permitted members of a convict's family to make regular visits? Other visitors needed specific permission from the minister of justice, did they not?

The justice minister replied, saying that was *supposed* to be the procedure. He claimed Warden Whyte had acted on his own, thereby breaking regulations. Bourke, he added, had done the same thing in subsequent meetings. The minister also admitted that the CPR detective had promised Miner a pardon if he returned the Australian securities, though the detective had not been empowered to implement this. The justice minister tried to dismiss the whole matter of an alleged pardon agreement. Since Miner had escaped, it was moot anyway, he said. Because of this fact, no effort to determine if the bonds had been located had subsequently been undertaken.

On March 2, Taylor crossed swords with the solicitor general again, and pointedly asked why the justice ministry had not asked the Australian government whether or not the securities had been returned. He read part of a February 12 article that had appeared in the *Vancouver Daily Province* into the parliamentary record.

"An official who is in the position to speak authoritatively," he read, had called the purported negotiations a ruse. "Certain persons made it possible for Miner to escape, apparently on the understanding that he would divide up the booty. These facts can easily be proved if the government makes an investigation."

That opened a new can of worms for the government. Had the guards engineered the escape just to share in Miner's loot? Other parliamentarians began calling for an inquiry with a fresh set of investigators who could not possibly be accused of involvement for personal gain, whether it was real or otherwise.

Finally, Prime Minister Sir Wilfred Laurier tried to put an end to the melee. "No more dangerous criminal, I think was ever in the clutches of Canadian justice," Laurier said, but he escaped and that was that. The prime minister flatly refused to open a full inquiry and the matter died forever. No one from the Canadian government was going to officially ask the Australians about whether the securities had been returned. It was also decided that no one had the right to meddle in the CPR's private business dealings with their customers. Miner had simply disappeared. The less said about the embarrassing matter, the better.

Chapter 10
Miner's Last Escape

omehow Bill Miner not only managed to escape the New Westminster prison, he also slipped out of Canada and crossed into the United States. It seems he arrived "home" undetected by the watchful army of Pinkerton's National Detective Agency, as well.

Miner traveled all the way to Pennsylvania under the alias of George Anderson and, at the age of 63, got a job in a sawmill looking after electrical equipment. He was a wiry 130 pounds and moved with slow determination through each day. George Anderson was generally viewed as a harmless old drifter, except to those he chose for private friendships.

True to his nature, one such friendship was with a young sawmill hand named Charles Hunter. As he had done in the past, Bill probably confessed his real identity to the impressionable youth. And most likely, with tales of adventure and high times, which he colorfully embellished, convinced the boy to travel south with him in search of a train to rob.

In Virginia, while Bill was celebrating his 64th birthday, the two met another aimless character named George Hansford. The trio settled in Lula, Georgia, where they took work in a local sawmill conveniently located near the main line of the Southern Express.

It didn't take Bill long. On February 12, 1911, he led his gang of inexperienced train robbers in flagging down the New Orleans-to-New York Southern Express at White Sulphur Springs, near Gainesville, Georgia. The train carried two safes. But Bill still had not perfected the art of blasting. Though he tried three times, he was only able to peel the door from the small safe to collect $1000 in booty. The large safe he repeatedly assaulted remained tightly closed, protecting $60,000 in gold. Nonetheless, with his dynamite, Bill managed to commit the first train robbery in the history of the State of Georgia.

One would think that after all his heists, Miner might have considered changing his methodology, particularly the parts of it that always ended up in his capture. Bill, however, was a creature of habit. Fleeing to the hills, Miner and his gang hid in the woods for several days before deciding to split up. The two younger men turned north, and Bill made his way south toward a town called Dahlonega by traveling under the cover of darkness.

When he found an abandoned cabin near Dahlonega, Miner decided to rest. It was there that the posse found Bill — sleeping peacefully. The description the posse was using to help identify the robbers was sketchy. Tired and discouraged by a fruitless hunt through the Georgia countryside, they almost passed Bill up. After all, the old man calling himself George Anderson was a cheery fellow, though he complained about ill health. However, because they'd had no success up to that point, the posse decided to search the cabin. They uncovered a mail-order gun, a bundle of money, and a pouch of jewels under a pillow on the cot where the old man had been sleeping. Miner acted completely confused by the fuss the posse made. He politely insisted the money and jewels belonged to him. He said he'd purchased the gun just as an old man's protection and had never even fired it. How would an old fellow like him manage to rob a train, anyway? The posse almost believed him, but decided to err on the side of caution. They helped the old-timer climb on a horse and delivered him to the Dahlonega jail.

Had it not been for the capture of his partners, who identified Bill as their co-conspirator, he may have been allowed to walk away from Dahlonega a free man. However, as he rested in the jail cell adamantly denying he knew the boys, Miner drew the attention of a Pinkerton's detective who'd been dispatched to investigate the train robbery. Bill Miner had continued to be one of the agency's most wanted criminals. Pinkerton's force had ignored reports that the outlaw had drowned or was still hiding in Canada. They regularly updated dispatches to their offices across the United States with his description. The most recent Pinkerton's detective remembered one of the old detailed alerts — and on an off chance — he checked old George Anderson for telltale tattoos.

The discovery that the tired posse had unknowingly caught Miner caused a sensation in Georgia. On March 11, 1911, the trial for the robbery was conducted with fanfare. Miner's accomplices had already pled guilty to their charges and though Miner had resolutely denied any participation in the robbery, he made a last minute bid for a lighter sentence by admitting his guilt. It didn't work. The boys were given 15-year sentences and Miner received 20 years confinement, to be served on the Milledgeville State Prison Farm.

Application was immediately made by Canadian authorities to return him to New Westminster to serve his life term there. Pinkerton's people, believing the country jail would be too easy for Miner to escape from, supported the extradition. Even Bill, who expected to receive harsh treatment in a Georgia chain gang, wanted to return to the north. But the Georgia officials would not hear of it. Bill Miner, who to them appeared old and sickly, was hardly a dangerous criminal by any stretch of the imagination. The outlaw was going to remain their prisoner and serve his sentence.

Bill did everything he could to support the impression that he was harmless. For six months he was a model prisoner in Milledgeville and his warders gradually relaxed their close observation. They shouldn't have.

On October 18, 1911, with another convict named Tom Moore, Bill managed to overpower a guard and escape. Even with his crippled feet, Bill and his young companion evaded searchers for 17 days. The two men were finally spotted in a train yard in St. Clair, Georgia, and the boxcar they were hiding in was quickly surrounded. Moore, who'd taken a gun from the Milledgeville guard, started firing. In answer, the posse riddled the boxcar with bullets. When Moore was fatally shot, Bill picked up the gun and continued to fire back at the posse until he ran out of bullets. Then, he calmly tossed out the gun and announced his surrender.

This time, when he was returned to the prison, his guards were more cautious. They outfitted Bill with a heavy ball and chain that he was forced to carry when he moved. That punishment, if nothing more, would have been enough reason for Bill to dream of another escape. On June 29, 1912, in the midst of a thunderstorm, Bill got his chance. He had somehow managed to cut through his shackles and to saw the bars on his cell during a noisy storm. With his two cellmates, W.M. Wiggins and W.J. Widencamp, he slipped from a second-story cell on a bed-sheet rope.

Instead of looking for an easy escape by train, however, Miner led the convicts to the Oconee River. Two days later they stole a small boat and headed into the Oconee swamp. Not far along, they capsized their tiny craft and Widencamp drowned. It left the other two alone to navigate in a foul-smelling swamp infested with poison snakes. Bill's poor sense of direction didn't serve him any better there than it had in the mountains of Colorado on one of his other runs to freedom. For three days the men traversed the miserable terrain, trying to cope with biting insects and without food or water. Miner, for all his grit, was no great physical specimen, so when a chance to leave the swamp presented itself, he leapt at it. The men tramped out of the swamp near Toomsboro, only about 18 miles from the prison. At the first farmhouse they found, they begged for a meal. The farmer, recognizing the two, gave the men a meal and called the Toomsboro sheriff. As Bill ate his first food in nearly a week, the Toomsboro lawmen swooped down on them.

Conducted back to Milledgeville in shackles, Bill was embarrassed to find a hero's welcome awaiting him. A large crowd had gathered and they cheered as the automobile that carried him back to prison passed through town.

Once back inside the Milledgeville doors, Bill was outfitted with ankle chains because he refused to promise he would not try to escape again. It was, however, rather pointless. Bill was tired and had grown quite weak. He was given a job tending the prison flower garden, the only job that didn't completely tax him physically. His health declined rapidly. In mid-August 1913, he suffered a gastric attack and was taken to the prison hospital. After weeks of lingering near death, he fell into a coma and at 9:25 p.m. on September 2, 1913, he quietly died.

Epilogue

As the authorities were unable to find any of Bill Miner's relatives, the old outlaw's body was marked for medical school experiments and would have been cut in pieces had it not been for Joseph Alfred Moore. "Mr. Joe," who owned the Milledgeville funeral parlor, had taught Sunday school classes to the men at the Milledgeville Prison. During his many visits, he'd built a friendship with the well-spoken bandit. As a private tribute to Bill, he bought a casket and provided a burial plot. Appealing to the townsfolk, he also raised enough donations to buy Bill his last new suit.

W.M. Pinkerton, head of the well-known detective agency, once referred to the mild-mannered quiet-spoken Miner as "... the master criminal of the American West." Moore made sure Bill got a send-off befitting that infamous title.

The funeral held in his funeral parlor was attended by hundreds of locals who filed by Bill's open casket for a last look. After a non-eulogistic service, prominent citizens of Milledgeville acted as Bill's pallbearers. Ironically, as though Bill was getting the last laugh, the mourners followed Moore's shiny black hearse away from the prison down Liberty Street to the cemetery on Memory Hill, where he was laid to rest on September 8, 1913.

Bill lay in his unmarked grave until 1964 when a noted

Georgia historian, Dr. James C Bonner, and some members of the Milledgeville Rotary Club, erected a tombstone. The engraved monument reads:

BILL MINER THE LAST OF THE FAMOUS WESTERN BANDITS. BORN 1843 DIED IN THE MILLEDGEVILLE STATE PRISON SEPT 2, 1914

Incredibly, the enigma Bill loved to embody throughout his life was given an extra dose of mystery in death. Both dates are wrong. He isn't even buried under that monument, but actually lies in an unmarked grave — No. 6 in lot 18 to the east — unless, of course, he managed to escape that final prison, too.

Further Reading

Anderson, Frank W. *Old Bill Miner Last of the Famous Western Bandits* Surrey, B.C.: Heritage House Publishing Company Ltd. 2001

Anderson, Frank W. *Bill Miner...Train Robber* Surrey, B.C.: Frontier Books, 1968

Boessenecker, John. *Badge and Buckshot: Lawlessness in Old California* Norman, Oklahoma: University of Oklahoma Press, 1988

Boessenecker, John and Dugan, Mark. *The Grey Fox: The True Story of Bill Miner Last of the Old-Time Bandits* Norman, Oklahoma: University of Oklahoma Press, 1992

Cawston, Verna B. "The Grey Fox goes to earth, again." Annual Report of the Okanagan Historical Society, 1984, 69-74

Dugan, Mark. *Bandit Years: A Gathering of Wolves* Santa Fe, New Mexico: Sunstone Press, 1987

Princeton History Book Committee. *Princeton Our Valley* Princeton, B.C.: 2000

Acknowledgments

The author would like to thank Phil Lepoidevin, summer student extraordinaire who led me through the bowels of the Princeton Museum archive and allowed me to wander undisturbed through decades of fragile old newspapers. And Mike, the Princeton old-timer who wouldn't divulge his last name but would, for the price of a cold beer, take me up the draw from downtown Princeton to the spot on Baldy where he said Jack Budd's cabin once sat (by the way, Mike, the fishing on Hook Lake was as great as you said it would be on the early rise). Thanks, too, to the ranchers and farmers who let me wander around Aspen Grove to get a feel for the country.

The author wishes to acknowledge the following newspapers and magazines for additional research and quotations:

Atlanta Constitution: March 5, 1911
Daily Columbian: Feb 27, 1909
Kamloops Standard: May 19, 1906
Scarlet and Gold, Vol 1: Dec 1919
Similkameen Star: May 19, 1906, April 15, 1948
Stockton Daily Evening Herald: March 2, 1866

About the Author

Stan Sauerwein lives and writes in Westbank, British Columbia. A freelance writer for two decades, Stan has written articles that have appeared in a variety of Canadian and U.S. magazines and newspapers. Specializing in business subjects, he has written for both corporations and governments. He is the author of seven other books — *Rattenbury: The Life and Tragic End of B.C.'s Greatest Architect, Ma Murray: The Story of Canada's Crusty Queen of Publishing, Klondike Joe Boyle: Heroic Adventures from Gold Fields to Battlefields, Moe Norman: The Canadian Golfing Legend with the Perfect Swing, Pierre Elliott Trudeau: The Fascinating Life of Canada's Most Flamboyant Prime Minister, Lucy Maud Montgomery: The Incredible Life of the Creator of Anne of Green Gables, Soapy Smith: Scourge of the Klondike,* and *Fintry: Lives, Loves and Dreams.*

Photo Credits

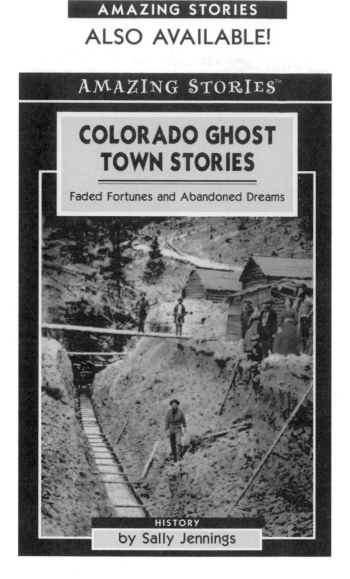
ISBN 1-55265-200-9